# WORLD'S GREATEST
# ★ MAGIC TRICKS ★

# WORLD'S GREATEST
## ★ MAGIC TRICKS ★

## CHARLES BARRY
## TOWNSEND

**Sterling Publishing Co., Inc.**
New York

*This book is dedicated to my son Mark for his perseverance and hard work in graduating from the University of Washington. We're all mighty proud of you.*

**Library of Congress Cataloging-in-Publication Data**

Townsend, Charles Barry.
  World's greatest magic tricks / by Charles Barry Townsend.
    p.  cm.
  Sequel to: World's best magic tricks. 1992.
  Includes index.
  ISBN 0-8069-0580-8
  1. Conjuring. 2. Tricks. I. Title.
  GV1547.T66    1994
  793.8--dc20                  94-12463
                                         CIP

10  9  8  7  6  5  4  3  2  1

Published in 2005 by Sterling Publishing Co., Inc.
387 Park Avenue South, New York, NY 10016
© 1994 by Charles barry Townsend
Distributed in Canada by Sterling Publishing
℅ Canadian Manda Group, 165 Dufferin Street,
Toronto, Ontario, Canada M6K 3H6
Distributed in Great Britain and Europe by Chris Lloyd at Orca Book
Services, Stanley House, Fleets Lane, Poole BH15 3AJ, England
Distributed in Australia by Capricorn Link (Australia) Pty. Ltd.
P.O. Box 704, Windsor, NSW 2756, Australia

Sterling ISBN  1-4027-2545-0

For information about custom editions, special sales, premium and
corporate purchases, please contact Sterling Special Sales
Department at 800-805-5489 or specialsales@sterlingpub.com.

# CONTENTS

# ROPE MAGIC

# MONEY MAGIC

# CARD MAGIC

# MISCELLANEOUS ITEMS

# INDEX

# INTRODUCTION

Hello again! It's great to be back with my second book devoted exclusively to magic. I hope you are among the numerous readers who found merit in *The World's Best Magic Tricks*. In that book I provided you with 48 of the very best tricks that have entertained magic lovers for over 100 years. Now, you are about to learn an additional 37 mysteries that you can add to your performing repertoire.

I've divided this book into eight sections: Silk Magic, Table Magic, Parlor Magic, Mental Magic, Paper Magic, Rope Magic, Money Magic, and Card Magic. Over 90 illustrations will help you to take the guesswork out of performing these masterpieces. You'll find that subtle secrets are the rule here. The emphasis is on presentation, not on sleight of hand.

Magic is one of the oldest forms of entertainment. Descriptions of conjuring performances in ancient Egypt date back to 3766 B.C. Every age has had its share of conjurers and men of mystery. Today, magic is thriving as never before. From causing railroad cars to disappear to flying into the theater and onto the stage, contemporary wizards are stretching the limits of credulity. You too can join their ranks by mastering the feats that are detailed within the pages of this book. Work hard and guard the secrets well! They are your key to becoming a Master of Mystery!

Charles Barry Townsend

# Silk Magic

## AN IMPOSSIBLE PENETRATION

### Effect

You start this effect by picking up and displaying an ordinary clear drinking glass. Holding it mouth-upward in your right hand, you push a bright red silk handkerchief down into it. You then take a plain white handkerchief and drape it over the top of the glass, hiding the glass from sight completely. Next, snap a rubber band around both the glass and the white handkerchief. The red handkerchief is thus safely sealed within the glass. You now reach underneath the white handkerchief and immediately bring your hand back out holding the red handkerchief. The rubber band and white handkerchief are then removed, revealing an empty glass. All items can immediately be passed around for examination. Once again, the impossible is proved to be commonplace in the hands of the master magician!

### Materials needed

One clear, straight-sided drinking glass • a white handkerchief • a red silk handkerchief • a rubber band.

### Presentation

Pick up the glass and hold it mouth-upward about chest-high. Then pick up the red handkerchief in your left hand and push it down into the glass (Fig. 1). Next, pick up the white handkerchief and bring it up in front of the glass. As you start to cover the glass, the right hand allows the glass to rotate downwards so that it is bottom-upward when covered by the handkerchief (Figs. 2 & 3). You now snap the rubber band around the top of the glass. To all appearances the red silk is now firmly imprisoned within the glass. Although the

Fig. 1

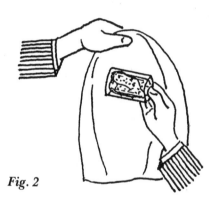

Fig. 2

Fig. 3

open end of the glass is facing downwards, the straight sides of it help to keep the red silk from falling out.

You now reach under the handkerchief, take hold of the red silk, and pull it straight down, giving the illusion that you

**Fig. 4**

are pulling it through the bottom of the glass (Fig. 4). You then drop the red silk onto the table and take hold of the white handkerchief above the rubber band. Your other hand goes back under the handkerchief and takes hold of the mouth of the glass. When the rubber band comes free of the glass, let the glass rotate on your fingertips. This action will, of course, be masked by the handkerchief until the glass is mouth-upward. The handkerchief is then removed and you can now pass the glass around for examination.

This is really a very startling trick, one that is straightforward, using simple, ordinary items. When well done, it has all the attributes of a minor miracle.

# Table Magic

## THE MAGNETIC PAPER CLIPS

### Effect

Display two jumbo paper clips, one in each hand, and say, "Static electricity is a remarkable force." "When properly understood it can endow any object with a positive or negative charge. As an example, if I rub the paper clip in my left hand against the cloth of my right sleeve I will impart a positive charge to the clip. In turn, if I rub the paper clip in my right hand against the cloth of my left sleeve I will impart a negative charge to the clip. This can easily be proved, since unlike charges attract. Watch this. I place the clip in my left hand down on the table. If I now touch it with the clip in my right hand the two should cling together if they have truly been charged. Yes, look at that! When I raise my right hand the two clips are stuck together. Amazing! Here are the paper clips. Let's see if you can magnetize them the way I did!"

At this point, open your hands and let the clips drop to the table. Your hands are empty. Try as they may, the onlookers will find it is impossible for them to turn the clips into magnets.

### Materials needed

Two jumbo paper clips • a safety pin • a two-foot length of elastic cord • a small bar magnet about one inch long • some sticky tape.

### Preparation

The secret to performing this trick is the use of a special gimmick. (A gimmick is an aid to performing a trick that your audience knows nothing about.) To make the gimmick you will need a short length of elastic cord. Fasten the bar magnet to one end of the cord with cellophane tape. Attach a safety pin to the other end of the cord (Fig. 1). Next, take the

Magnet        Elastic        Safety Pin

**Fig. 1**

cord and insert it, magnet-end first, down the right sleeve of your jacket until the magnet is about two inches from the end of the sleeve (Fig. 2). Take the safety pin on the other end of

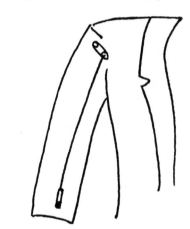

**Fig. 2**

the cord and attach it to the inside of your jacket at the point where it enters the sleeve. Put the jacket on and you're ready to perform this neat little mystery.

## Presentation

At some point in your presentation, when the attention of your audience is directed elsewhere, drop your hands below the tabletop and reach into your right sleeve with your left hand and pull the bar magnet down into your right hand

**12**

*Fig. 3*

(Fig. 3). Now, place your right hand, palm down, on top of the table while you reach into your side pocket with your left hand and bring forth the two jumbo paper clips. Drop one of them on the table and place the other clip into your right hand so that the end of the clip is up against the end of the magnet (Fig. 4). The clip is now magnetized and can be used

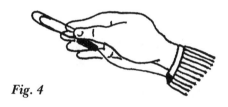

*Fig. 4*

to pick up the paper clip on the table. Hold the clips above the table for a few moments and then work the magnet away from touching the paper clip. The attracted paper clip will fall to the table. While all eyes are following this clip, the fingers of the right hand release their hold on the magnet, causing it to be drawn up into the sleeve and out of sight. Try as they may, your audience will fail to duplicate your electrifying feat.

This trick is a great lead-in to that classic stumper "The Linking Paper Clip Puzzle." Borrow a dollar bill from a member of your audience and say, "I'll wager this dollar that I can toss these two paper clips into the air and cause them to become linked together before they land on top of the table. Do I have any takers?"

The solution to this problem is simple. All you have to do is to take the dollar bill, fold it into thirds and insert the paper clips in the positions shown in Fig. 5. Now, grasp the bill by both ends and smartly snap it apart. The paper clips will fly into the air and land on the table firmly linked together. Another wager won!

*Fig. 5*

# THE FLOATING SALT SHAKER

## Effect

The following dinner-table effect, when properly done, has all the power of a minor miracle. After the main course has been completed and everyone is relaxing for a few minutes before the onslaught of dessert, bring up the subject of levitation as performed by the great magicians of the theater. Mention that your grandfather learned the secret of this trick from the great Houdini and that he passed it on to you when you were a young sprout. By way of illustration you stand up and place the glass salt shaker on the table in front of you. Extending the fingers of your right hand, lower them until the tips touch the top of the shaker (see Fig. 1). Now,

*Fig. 1*

very slowly, raise your hand about four or five inches. Miraculously, the salt shaker clings to your fingers and rises with them. Spread your fingers apart until the shaker is seen to be touching only your middle finger (see Fig. 2). Still it doesn't

*Fig. 2*

fall. After a few seconds, lower your hand until the shaker is once more resting on the table. Now open your hand and turn it around so that your audience can see it is empty. The shaker can immediately be examined.

## Materials needed

One salt shaker • a wooden toothpick • some sticky tape • a length of elastic cord.

## Preparation

This trick is performed with the aid of a clever gimmick that is unknown to your audience. Using the sticky tape, attach one end of the elastic to the toothpick. The toothpick should be of the round type that is pointed at both ends. The elastic should be about two feet long and have a safety pin attached to the other end. (This gimmick is similar to the one described in the previous trick, "The Magnetic Paper Clips.") Lower the toothpick end of the elastic down the right sleeve of your jacket until the toothpick is within one inch of the cuff. With the safety pin, attach the other end to the inside of your coat.

## Presentation

Before starting this trick you must secretly pull the toothpick out of your sleeve and hold it against your middle finger with your right thumb. You are now ready to start the mystery. Begin by talking about the many great magicians of history who performed the famous "floating lady" illusion. Reach forward, pick up the salt shaker, and place it in front of you on the table. It's best to be seated at the head of the table so that you will not have anyone at your sides who might glimpse the gimmick in your right hand. Stand up and bring your right hand forward with the back of it towards your audience. Bring the tips of your fingers down until they touch the top of the salt shaker as shown in Figure 1. At this point push the tip of the toothpick down into one of the holes in the middle of the metal cap until it's wedged in tightly. You are now ready to perform the trick described above.

At the end of the levitation, when the salt shaker is again resting on the table, wiggle the toothpick free from the metal cap and let the elastic pull it up into your sleeve. Show your hand back and front and give the shaker out for inspection.

In the impromptu version of this trick the magician dispenses with the elastic, tape, and safety pin and uses only the toothpick. At the end of the presentation he has to palm the toothpick and get rid of it while passing the shaker for examination. I think the method that employs the gimmick is the cleaner of the two versions.

# A PAPER AND PENCIL GAME

## Effect

This effect is designed to reinforce the perception of your mastery of numbers. It's a game which you can't lose, regardless of whether your opponent goes first or you do. During play, each of the two players writes down a number from 1 to 10. That number is added to the previous total of numbers as you go along. The players take turns writing down the numbers. The goal is to be the one who causes the total to reach exactly 100.

For example, let's say you go first and write down 5. The other player now writes a 9 under it and adds it up, giving a running total of 14. Now it's your turn again. You write a 9 under the 14, draw a line under it, and write down the new total of 23. Play continues in this fashion until someone writes down a number which brings the new total to exactly 100. When you know the secret to this mental exercise you will be unbeatable.

## Materials needed

Pencil and paper.

## Presentation

The secret lies in memorizing a group of key numbers. They are: 12, 23, 34, 45, 56, 67, 78, and 89. Please note that each number is 11 greater than the previous number. During play, you must cause the total to be one of these key numbers. Once you've done that you're assured of winning. From that point on always make sure that your number plus the previous number put down by your opponent add up to 11. This will ensure that every time you add a number to the previous total the new total will be one of the key numbers mentioned above.

When you get to the last key number, 89, you are a sure winner.

Another coup for the master mentalist!

# AN EASY NUMBER TRICK

## Effect

Hand a spectator a small pad and pencil. Request the spectator to write down any five-digit number that has five different numbers. Then ask your spectator to reverse the number and subtract the smaller of the two numbers from the larger. Once this is done, have the spectator reverse the result and add this new number to it. Instruct the spectator to concentrate on this number while you attempt to read his mind. After a moment or two, claim to be getting some faint impressions of the calculated number. "Yes, it's all becoming quite clear now. The number you are thinking of is . . . 109,890! Is that correct? It is! You have a very strong mind. Your thoughts came through loud and clear!"

## Materials needed

A pad and pencil.

## Preparation

None.

## Presentation

Just follow the description of the effect and it will work itself. The answer will almost always be 109,890. Suppose the first number written down by the spectator was 5 9 3 7 1. Reversing that gives 1 7 3 9 5. Subtracting the smaller number from the larger gives:

$$
\begin{array}{r}
5\ \ 9\ \ 3\ \ 7\ \ 1 \\
-\ 1\ \ 7\ \ 3\ \ 9\ \ 5 \\
\hline
4\ \ 1\ \ 9\ \ 7\ \ 6
\end{array}
$$

Reversing this number and adding the new number to it gives:

```
      4   1   9   7   6
  +   6   7   9   1   4
  1   0   9   8   9   0
```

This works almost every time. On occasion, however, the result will turn out to be 99,099. If it ever happens that the number is not 109,890, pretend that you must have intercepted someone else's thoughts. Tell your spectator to concentrate again on the number. Wait a moment and then announce that the number is 99,099.

# Parlor Magic

## THE BLOCK OFF THE RIBBON FEAT

### Effect

Show the audience a solid block of wood with a hole drilled through the center. In the other hand display a small wooden frame into which you slide the block. The frame has two matching holes on opposite sides that line up with the hole in the block. Pick up a long knitting needle that has a five-foot length of brightly colored ribbon attached to it. Using the needle, thread the ribbon through the frame and the block. After pulling the ribbon backward and forward a few times to show that the block is securely trapped within the wooden frame, hand the ends of the ribbon to two people from the audience to hold (Fig. 1). Now take the block and frame in your hands and, in full view of the audience, pull the block free of the restraining ribbon. All the items can immediately be passed around for examination.

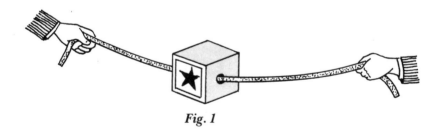

*Fig. 1*

### Materials needed

One solid wooden cube • one wooden frame • a five-foot length of colored three-quarter-inch ribbon • a spool of heavy black thread • beeswax or other soft wax • a knitting needle.

## Preparation

The wooden cube should measure around three inches to the side. A three-quarter-inch hole is drilled through the center of the cube. The frame is made of ⅝-inch stock and is three inches wide. The interior of the frame should be slightly larger than the cube. The insides and outsides of the frame should be painted black. The front and back edges of the frame can be painted red. The cube is either varnished or painted a bright contrasting color.

While the cube, ribbon, and frame are all perfectly genuine, the secret of the trick is in the use of a piece of black thread. Tie a large loop in the end of the thread and attach it to the inside of the frame. This loop goes around one of the holes in the frame, and the thread continues down along the side, across the bottom, up the other side, and out the opposite hole. The thread is kept in place with tiny bits of wax (Fig. 2). The rest of the thread, about five feet or so, hangs down. The end of this thread is attached to the floor or to the front edge of a heavy table.

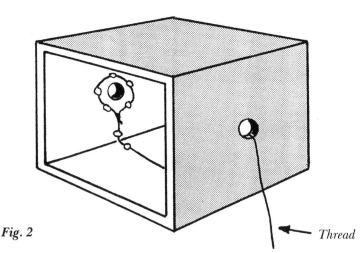

**Fig. 2**                                                   *Thread*

## Presentation

Let's say you're using a heavy table to hold your paraphernalia and the black thread is attached to the right front side of the table. Pick up and display the cube and frame. Slip the cube into the frame and show that the hole in the cube lines up with the holes in the frame. Now thread the ribbon through the frame, securely locking the cube within. Remove the needle from the ribbon and slide the ribbon back and forth through the frame and block a few times. While doing this, hold the frame and block in your right hand. Hold them in such a way that one of the holes in the frame faces the audience with the ribbon hanging out. With your left hand reach in front of the frame, grip the ribbon, and pull it down a few feet. Then reach in the back of the frame, grip the ribbon there, and pull it back down on that side. The second time you do this, with the end of the ribbon in the back of the frame, press down on the strip of ribbon in front of the frame so it is held tightly against the frame. Do this with your right middle finger. With your left hand lightly take hold of the ribbon in the back of the frame (Fig. 3). Just

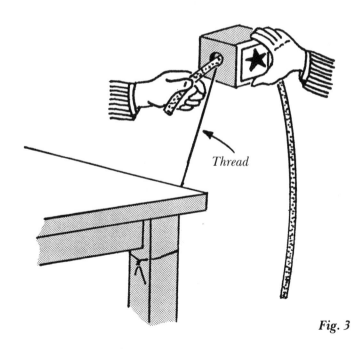

*Thread*

**Fig. 3**

as you're about to pull the ribbon down with this hand, move your body forward and away from the table. This action will cause the loop of thread inside the frame to take hold of the ribbon and pull the end of it (that part that is in back of the frame) back through the hole in the block and then to go around between the block and the frame and finally come back out the hole again into your left hand (see Fig. 4). The

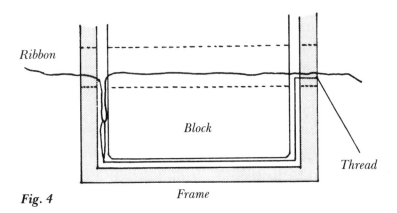

**Fig. 4**         *Frame*

left hand immediately pulls the ribbon down in back. You then pull the front part of the ribbon down for the last time, bringing the two ends of the ribbon together. At this point the loop of thread will have fallen to the floor where it will go unnoticed.

You are now ready to have the members of the audience take hold of the ends of the ribbon prior to the climactic conclusion of the trick. The success of this mystery is wholly dependent on the smooth execution of the move where the thread pulls the ribbon around the block and out the back of the frame. It should look as though you are merely pulling the ribbon back and forth a few times to show that everything is nice and secure. The movement of your body away from the table, along with your arm and hand movements, should effectively hide the secret from the audience during the split second of execution. Practise this move. Once mastered, it is a very perplexing illusion to add to your act.

# THE WONDERFUL PRODUCTION BOX

## Effect

Call attention to a brightly decorated box sitting on a small table. Remove the lid and, after showing it on both sides, place it on the table next to the box. Picking up the box, bring it forward so the audience can see that it is quite empty and that nothing is attached to the sides and bottom. Pick up the lid, put the box back on the table, and then replace the lid on it. Now the action begins. After rolling up your sleeves and making a few mystic passes over and around the box, proceed to remove a great number of articles that have suddenly and mysteriously materialized within its confines. Produce a large number of flags and silks, hundreds of paper flowers, and even a live bird or two. The box proves to be a veritable cornucopia of colorful and unusual items. Let's see how it's done!

## Materials needed

A plywood box with lid • a special bag for holding the items to be produced from the box • the production items (flags, scarves, paper flowers, birds, etc.)

## Preparation

Both the box and the lid should be made of plywood and should be brightly decorated. The inside of the box should be a light color so the audience can easily see that it is empty when shown the inside (Fig. 1).

The bag, which is to contain the items for the production, should be about eight inches in diameter. The top of it should have a series of eyelets sewn into the cloth around the top of the opening so the bag can be closed with a drawstring. Attach a short wire handle with a ring at the end to the top of the bag. The ring should be large enough for your middle finger to slide into easily. Just below this ring is a smaller ring

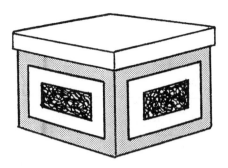

*Fig. 1*

that fits over a nail that supports the bag in the back of the table (Fig. 2).

*Fig. 2*

There should be a ten-inch drape running around the four sides of the table. This is so the audience cannot see the bag when it is hanging down in the back of the table (Fig. 3).

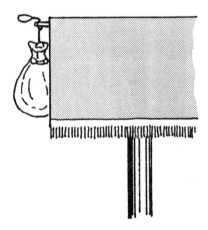

*Fig. 3*

## Presentation

Stand behind the table and remove the lid from the box. Show all sides of it and then, taking it in your right hand, pick up the box with your left hand and place the lid down on the back of the table so the edge of the lid hangs over for about three-quarters of an inch. The wire ring from the bag should be centered on the back edge of the lid.

Tilt the opening of the box towards the audience so everyone can see that the box is empty. Turning back to the table reach down with your right hand and pick up the lid. In doing so insert your right middle finger into the wire loop attached to the bag and pick it up with the lid (Fig. 4). The lid

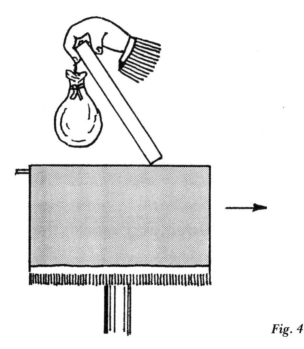

*Fig. 4*

will conceal the bag from the view of the audience. Make sure the outside top of the lid is perpendicular to the floor.

Replace the box on the table. Take hold of the bottom of the lid with your left hand and bring the lid over and to the front of the box. Place the bottom of the lid over the front edge of the box and tilt the lid back and down until it fits snugly over the box (Fig. 5). During this action the bag will be lowered into the box and the wire hanger will slip off your finger.

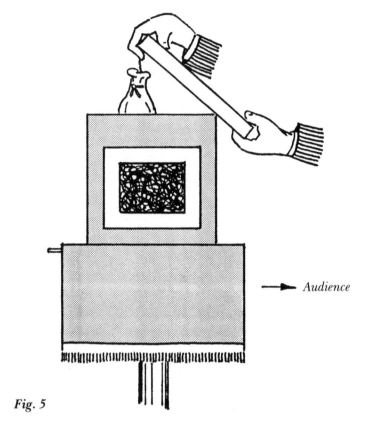

Audience

**Fig. 5**

From your point of view the trick is over. All you need to do now is utter the magic words and start producing the items concealed in the bag.

ringing bell and the various objects tossed over the top of the banner.

At the conclusion of the performance turn to your right to place the banner back on the table, and turn the banner rod inward and down in such a manner that the banner furls itself around the dummy hand. Drop your gloved right hand and catch the right-bottom corner of the banner and continue this furling action. When done smoothly it will appear that you took your right hand off of the rod and used it to furl the banner around the rod.

You will probably want to elaborate on the presentation given here. Dimming the lights and playing ghostly music would certainly add to the performance. You might want to play this séance for comedy, giving away the secret at the end by putting your gloved right hand on the center of the rod, thus showing three hands holding up the banner. This séance can be extremely entertaining, so practise it well and include it in your next show.

# A MIND-OVER-MATTER EXHIBITION

## Effect

State that you are about to give a conclusive exhibition of the very real powers of the mind. After commenting on the science of psychokinesis, the ability to move objects with thought alone, offer to duplicate some of the claims that have been reported. Say that you will need the help of members of the audience. Bring forward a heavy table and place several chairs around it. Four or five members of the audience are invited to come forward and sit around the table with you. Line up three bottles across the center of the table (Fig. 1). The bottles are each a different size and each is corked. A hole has been drilled through the center of each cork and

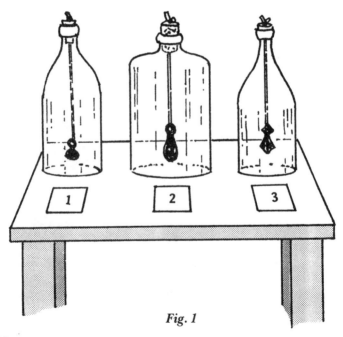

*Fig. 1*

cords run through into the bottles. At the end of each cord is a lead fishing weight. These weights act as pendulums within the bottles and can swing back and forth freely. The other ends of the cords are knotted at the tops of the corks. The bottles are numbered 1, 2, and 3.

Sit down in a chair facing the three bottles and place your hands on top of the table with your fingertips resting on it. Ask for complete silence in the room and instruct the spectators, seated around the table, to concentrate on making the weight in the middle jar swing. Slowly, at first, and then more rapidly, the weight begins to move. Although no movement on the performer's part is observed, the weight swings wider and wider while the weights in the other two bottles remain motionless.

After a few seconds, instruct the spectators to shift their thoughts from the weight in the middle bottle to the weight in bottle one. Slowly the middle weight stops its swinging motion and then the weight in bottle one begins to move. After a few moments, call on the people at the table to shift their concentration to bottle three, where the same results are obtained.

To prove that the manifestations just witnessed were not the work of trickery, ask one of the spectators to take your place at the table. Once again the same results are obtained. First one weight is set in motion, then another, and so on. The spectators will be amazed as they each take their turn and find that they too are able to concentrate the powers of the assembled minds over the inert objects in the bottles.

## Materials needed

Three bottles of different sizes • three corks, string, and fishing weights (the weights should be of different sizes) • a firm table • five or six chairs.

## Presentation

Place numbered cards in front of the bottles. Drill a hole through the top of each cork and then thread each with a string. Triple-knot the ends of the cords so they will not slide through the holes. Attach a lead weight to the end of each cord. Make sure that when each weight is lowered into a bottle, and the cork is driven home, the weight hangs about two or three inches from the bottom of the bottle. Each weight must be able to swing about freely inside the bottle.

## Presentation

There are no tricks associated with the workings of this mystery. Precede as described above until you come to the placing of the fingertips on the tabletop. The weights are made to move by applying pressure to the table with the tips of your fingers. All that it takes is a subtle pressing and relaxing of the fingers in time with the swing weight. However, this action must be so slight that it is not perceivable to those who are watching you. To do this you must relax and concentrate completely on one weight at a time. Because each is a different weight, only one at a time will respond to your controlled pressures on the table. Just stare at the weight and *will it* to move. Your body will pick up the tempo and do the rest.

To stop a moving weight, just concentrate on stopping it. When it slows down, switch your thoughts to another bottle and make that weight start to move. Practise this first with one bottle until you're able to control it completely. When one of the spectators takes your place at the table, guide him along with suggestions on how to concentrate on one weight at a time and how to lightly, but firmly, place his fingertips upon the table. Practise this aspect of the performance with your family and friends until you've developed the knack of getting successful results from strangers trying this experiment for the first time.

This is a formidable demonstration of supposed mental abilities and lends itself to all kinds of story and plot lines. It's up to you to sell this feat as good, interesting pseudo-scientific entertainment.

# Mental Magic

## THE GREAT CALENDAR MYSTERY

### Effect

Announce that you, the Mental Marvel, can, under certain test conditions, demonstrate the gift of second sight. A member of the audience is called forward to assist you. Show four large pages from the current year's calendar and request the assistant to choose one and place it on an easel. Turn your back to the easel and request the assistant to blindfold you. Explain that you want the volunteer to circle one day in each of the five weeks of the selected calendar month. To make sure the selection of days is perfectly random, request that members of the audience shout out days of the week. As each day is shouted, the assistant circles a date under it on the calendar. Different dates for the same day of the week can be circled, but only one date per *week* is circled. As the last date is circled, dramatically announce that you see a number in your mind that represents the total of the five numbers just selected. After saying the number, remove the blindfold and instruct the volunteer to write the five numbers on the side of the board and add them up. The total will, of course, match the one you give. An impressive test of mental ability!

### Materials

One large easel • four pages from a current calendar (they must be months that contain five Wednesdays) • four large, clear plastic sheets to cover the calendar pages • a magic marker.

### Preparation

First, find the largest size calendar available and remove all the months that contain five Wednesdays. Depending on the year, there will be either three or four such months. Mount each of these on a large sheet of bristol board. The bristol board should be six inches wider than the calendar sheets so a section on the right side of each board can be reserved for writing down the five dates for summing.

You have two options about how to mark the calendars. You can cover a calendar with a plastic sheet and write on it with erasable magic marker. Or, you can give the volunteer a pad of "sticky" note pads, the type that have pages that are easily removable from whatever they are attached to. This way, the numbers are duly noted on the calendar and you don't have to mess around with clear overlays and magic markers. You will, however, have to affix a fresh strip of paper down the right side of the bristol board every time you perform this trick so the numbers can be added up.

## Presentation

And now for the modus operandi of this interesting example of second sight. The secret lies in knowing a key number associated with each month used in the experiment. The key number is arrived at by adding up the five dates in the Wednesday column of the calendar month and memorizing these numbers. In Figure 1 the total is 85. The key numbers for the months used in 1994 are: March = 80; June = 75; August = 85; November = 80. In 1995, they are: March = 75; May = 75; August = 80; November = 75. You must also memorize the numerical values that are assigned to each day of the week. Sunday equals − 3, Monday equals − 2, Tuesday equals − 1, Wednesday equals 0, Thursday equals 1, Friday equals 2, and Saturday equals 3.

Once this information has been memorized, it becomes an easy matter to calculate the sum of the dates mentally. Using the key value of the selected month as a starting point (85 in our example), simply add the value for each day to it as the days are shouted out. In our case when Monday was called, two was subtracted from 85, giving 83; when Tuesday was called, one was subtracted from 83, giving 82; when Wednes-

**Fig. 1**

day was called, nothing was subtracted; when Thursday was selected, one was added to 82, giving 83; and finally, when Saturday was called out, three was added to 83, giving 86. At this point, announce that the total of the five dates is 86 and request the volunteer to confirm this by writing down the five dates on the side of the board and adding them up.

This is an excellent mental feat for stage or parlor. You can also perform this close up. Get a small calendar, remove the months needed to perform the feat, and glue them to a sheet of typing paper. Photocopy a few sheets and you're ready to present this mental gem at the table. Hand the sheet to someone and turn your back while the person selects any five dates from one of the months. This presentation is basically the same as the stage version.

# ANOTHER GREAT CALENDAR MYSTERY

## Effect

In this test you, the Mental Marvel, demonstrate your abilities as a lightning calculator. Pass out a small yearly calendar to anyone sitting in the first row. Instruct this person to tear out a sheet for any month and then to pass the calendar to the next two people in the row, who should also select any month and remove the pages from the calendar. Request the first person to circle any box of nine days in the month he selected. The box must contain three days across and three days down (Fig. 1, left). Tell this person to add up the numbers in the four corner squares of the box and to state what the total is. (In our example the sum is 80.) Then tell the first person to concentrate on the number in the middle of the square. After a brief pause, announce that the number in the square is 20.

Request the second member of the audience to make a box from any three vertical days on the calendar month (Fig. 1, middle). Instruct this individual to sum up the three dates circled and give you the total. Upon hearing the number, instantly tell the spectator what three numbers were picked.

Tell the third person to circle any four days on the calendar month to form a square, two days across and two days down (Fig. 1, right), and to add up all four numbers in the square and tell you the total. As soon as you hear what the total is, name the four selected numbers. Three for three, the master of mystery is batting a thousand!

## Materials needed

One desk-sized calendar, say four inches by six inches • three pencils.

# 1994  JUNE

| SUN | MON | TUES | WED | THURS | FRI | SAT |
|-----|-----|------|-----|-------|-----|-----|
|     |     |      | 1   | 2     | 3   | 4   |
| 5   | 6   | 7    | 8   | 9●    | 10  | 11  |
| 12  | 13  | 14   | 15  | 16'   | 17  | 18  |
| 19  | 20  | 21   | 22  | 23    | 24  | 25  |
| 26  | 27  | 28   | 29  | 30'   |     |     |

*Fig. 1*

## Presentation

There is no setup for this trick. Just pass out the calendar and the pencils and you're ready to go. The three spectators can choose any of the twelve months on the calendar. Let's start with the first problem: using nine numbers. In the example shown in Figure 1, the sum of the four corner squares is 80. All that is needed to calculate the value of the center square is to divide this sum by 4, which gives us 20, the number we are looking for.

Another effect that you can do with a block of nine numbers is to ask the value of the lowest number in the block.

When the person tells you, immediately say what the total is for all nine numbers in the block. Do this by adding 8 to the number and then multiplying the result by 9. The fastest way to do this in your head is to multiply the result by 10 and then subtract the number multiplied from the result. For example, the lowest number is 12. Add 8 to it, to get 20. Multiply this by 10, to get 200, and subtract 20 (the number multiplied), to get the correct answer, 180.

Now, let's move on to the second problem. In this example the spectator adds three numbers, in this case, 16, 23, and 30, and tells you the total is 69. You divide this number by 3, giving you 23, the middle number of the three. Subtract 7, giving you 16, the top number. Finally, add 7 to the 23, giving you 30, the bottom number.

The solution to the four-number puzzle is similar to the last one. In the example, the total of the four numbers is 28. To find the first of these numbers, divide the total by 4 and then subtract 4 from the result. Divide 28 by 4, giving 7, and then subtract 4, to arrive at 3, the first, and the lowest, of the four numbers. Add 1, to get 4, the second number. Next, add 6, to get 10, the third number. Finally, add 1, to get 11, the fourth number.

This is a neat exercise in mental gymnastics that you can perform anywhere when called upon to show an example of your mental powers.

# THE AMAZING LICENSE PLATE PREDICTION

## Effect

Point to the back of the stage, where a ribbon stretches from one side to the other. Suspended from the center of the ribbon is a large, brown business envelope. The envelope hangs about eight feet above the floor. State that the envelope contains a prediction you made before the show began concerning the experiment in precognition that you are about to conduct with the help of the audience. "The first thing we have to do is to create a license plate number. I'm going to toss this Ping-Pong ball out into the audience and the person who catches it will choose the state." When the state has been selected, write the two-letter abbreviation for it on the blackboard.

"Now that we have the state, let's add four digits to it. Will the person who caught the Ping-Pong ball please toss it into the air so another person can pick the first number?" The person who catches the ball picks a number from zero to nine and you write it next to the state abbreviation on the board. The ball is then tossed to another part of the audience. In this manner three more numbers are chosen at random and written down.

When this is done, point to the board and state, "Here we have our license plate. It was created using the selections of five randomly chosen people in our audience. For me to have known, in advance, what the outcome of this experiment would be is patently an impossibility. And yet . . . stranger things have happened. Let's see what I wrote down and sealed in the envelope that has been in full sight of all of you good people since tonight's entertainment began." (Figure 1 shows the blackboard with the prediction hanging in the background and an example of the type of license plate number that the audience will create.)

Place a chair under the ribbon, step up on it, and cut the

ribbon on both sides of the envelope. Step down and walk towards the front of the stage, where you snip off one end of

*Fig. 1*

the envelope, reach inside, and remove a second sealed envelope. You immediately hand this envelope to a member of the audience to open. Inside is found a folded sheet of paper that, when opened up, has a picture of a license plate drawn on it with the same state abbreviation and four numbers that were selected by the various members of the audience under seemingly test conditions.

Is this an example of genuine precognition? Read on and find out.

## Materials needed

A large brown envelope, say about 11 inches by 8 inches • a brown business-size envelope • a long length of one-inch-wide red ribbon • a large sheet of white paper • a sturdy chair • an envelope holder to be attached to the back of the chair • a Ping-Pong ball • a black felt-tipped marking pen • a chalkboard or other type of large free-standing easel to write on.

## Preparation

Before your performance begins you must seal the large brown envelope and attach it to the center of the length of ribbon. You then fasten the ends of the ribbon to the curtains on both sides of the stage. The envelope should hang about eight feet above the stage and to the back of it. It should, however, be well away from the rear curtain.

The chair used when cutting down the envelope should be quite sturdy. Although the back of the chair should be open, the top rail must be quite deep, say around eight to ten inches. This is to hide the small prediction envelope that is contained in the envelope holder that is fastened to the back of the chair with strips of adhesive tape (Fig. 2). The holder is made with thick pieces of cardboard and bristol board. The envelope should fit loosely inside the holder.

The chair is placed well to the side of the stage. The back of the chair must be hidden from the view of the audience.

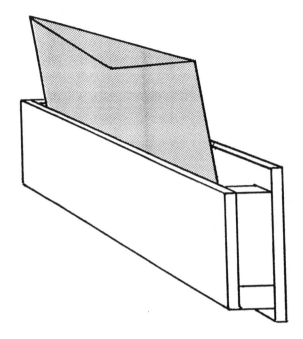

*Fig. 2*

## Presentation

There is one other item you need in order to perform this feat: a hidden assistant, who doesn't even have to be hidden, just out of sight for a minute or two. The floor plan illustrates the stage layout (Fig. 3). The brown prediction envelope is

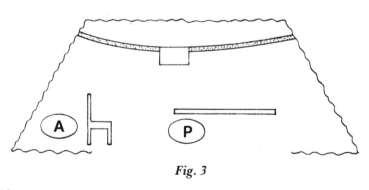

*Fig. 3*

hanging to the rear of the stage, the magician is front and center by his blackboard, the chair is to the left partially hidden, and in back of it, completely hidden, is the assistant. The presentation follows along the lines previously stated. As each element of the license plate number is created, you write it down on the board; the assistant is also writing the same information with the black felt-tipped marking pen on a pre-folded sheet of white paper. As soon as the last digit has been called out, the assistant writes it down, folds up the sheet, and seals it in the small brown envelope. He then slips the envelope into the envelope holder on the back of the chair.

While the assistant is doing this, you have been summing up your actions to this point and have once again drawn the audience's attention to the large brown envelope hanging from the ribbon. Now either move the chair yourself, or request your assistant to come forward and position the chair under the hanging envelope. Step up onto the chair, remove a pair of scissors from your pocket, and cut the envelope free from the ribbon. Now comes the critical move. As you step down from the chair, place your right hand, which is holding the envelope, on the top rail of the chair to steady yourself. In doing so, hold the envelope tightly with the thumb and first finger of your hand. The envelope should be in *front* of the rail, in plain sight of the audience. The heel of your right hand is on the top of the rail and takes the weight of the descent. Meanwhile, the third, fourth, and fifth fingers of the right hand are behind the rail. At this moment the third and fourth fingers are clipping the top edge of the small brown envelope in the holder (Fig. 4). The envelope should be about half an inch below the top of the rail and should be leaning away from the rail about three-quarters of an inch. As you complete your descent from the chair remove your hand from the top rail, carrying the small envelope away, hidden behind the large envelope.

As you walk to the front of the stage shift the two envelopes as one to your left hand. Removing the scissors from your

*Fig. 4*

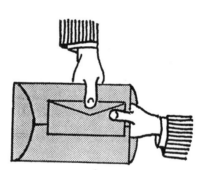

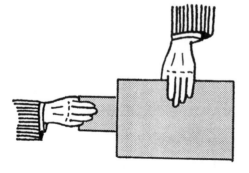

*Fig. 5*

pocket, cut off the end of the large envelope. The fingers of your right hand go into the envelope while the thumb remains outside, gripping the small envelope. Pull the small envelope to the right, where it appears to the audience as if it was being withdrawn from the inside of the large envelope (Fig. 5). All that is left to be done is to hand the small envelope to a member of the audience for the disclosure of the prediction.

One final note: As I mentioned above, the critical movement of the trick is capturing the small envelope with the third and fourth fingers of your right hand when it is resting on the top of the chair rail. You must practise this movement over and over again until you can do it while looking at your audience. Hard practice will reward you with an unbeatable prediction.

# MIND READING MADE EASY

## Effect

While idly shuffling a deck of cards mention that you have been having great success of late with a series of telepathic experiments. "With the aid of five spectators from the audience I would like to demonstrate my powers in the area of mind reading." When the five people take their positions around the table, spread the cards face-up and remark that the deck has been well shuffled for the test. Gathering up the cards, square the deck and place it on the table and invite anyone of the five spectators to cut it. When the cut is complete ask, "Is one cut enough? Would anyone else like to cut the cards?" Allow anyone who answers "yes" to cut the deck. Go on in this manner for two, three, or more cuts until all are satisfied.

Then instruct one of the spectators to remove the top five cards from the deck. Tell that person to mix the cards up without revealing their faces and to hand one to each of the other spectators and to retain one. Everyone is now told to concentrate on his card. After a few seconds, state that you are receiving thought waves of the identities of the cards. One by one, call out the identity of the cards. As each card is revealed, ask the member of the audience holding that card to turn it face outward so the audience can see it. This is a mental masterpiece that you can perform!

## Materials needed

One deck of 52 playing cards.

## Preparation

The secret of this mystery lies in a secret setup of the deck called "The Si Stebbins Set-Up." Si Stebbins was an outstanding magician who performed during the early part of this century. He came up with an extremely clever way of setting up a deck so that the conjurer would know the order of every single card in it. To set the deck up, take any card and place it face-up on the table. On top of this card place a card whose value is *three* more than the first card. Continue in this way until all the cards are on the pile. Face cards count: jack = 11, queen = 12, and king = 13. If a jack is face-up, then the next card would be an ace. If a queen is face-up, then the next would be a two, and so on. Also, to give the appearance of a well-shuffled deck the suits of the cards are rotated as they are placed down. First clubs, then hearts, then spades, and then, finally, diamonds. To make it easy to remember the order of the suits, visualize the word "Chased." The order of certain letters in the word correspond to the order of the suits in the setup. Think of the word like this: "**CHaSeD**." The capital letters stand for "clubs, hearts, spades, and diamonds."

Although you can start setting up your deck with any card, we give you an example of a complete deck starting with the ace of clubs:

A♣, 4♥, 7♠, 10♦, K♣, 3♥, 6♠, 9♦, Q♣, 2♥, 5♠, 8♦, J♣, A♥, 4♠, 7♦, 10♣, K♥, 3♠, 6♦, 9♣, Q♥, 2♠, 5♦, 8♣, J♥, A♠, 4♦, 7♣, 10♥, K♠, 3♦, 6♣, 9♥, Q♠, 2♦, 5♣, 8♥, J♠, A♦, 4♣, 7♥, 10♠, K♦, 3♣, 6♥, 9♠, Q♦, 2♣, 5♥, 8♠, J♦.

## Presentation

With the setup in the above Si Stebbins manner you can always know the value of any card above or below any known card. As an example, if you caught a glimpse of the bottom card of the above deck setup, the jack of diamonds, you would immediately be able to say that the top card of the deck is the ace of clubs. Remember the suit after "diamonds" in the word "CHaSeD" is clubs, and the next value after a jack is three higher, an ace.

Another thing to remember about this setup is that although you can't shuffle the deck, for this would destroy the setup, you can cut it any number of times without disturbing the order. Because of this restriction it's best to use this mind-reading trick as the opening one of your presentation. If you use it later on, you'll have to switch the deck you've been using for a prepared one with the Si Stebbins setup.

To perform the mind-reading mystery described above, pick up the deck after the spectator has removed the top five cards from it. While the spectator is busy mixing the cards and handing them out to the other four members of the audience, casually get a glimpse of the bottom card. Knowing the value of this card gives you the information needed to calculate what the value of the next five cards would be in the Si Stebbins setup. These would be the five cards that the spectator removed from the top of the deck. From this point on it's up to the performer to give a convincing demonstration of mind reading while revealing the values of the cards.

This is probably the best card deck setup ever invented. You should be able to create many other mysteries using this clever secret.

# A DEMONSTRATION OF EXTRASENSORY PERCEPTION

## Effect

"Tonight I'm going to present you with a demonstration of extrasensory perception," you exclaim. "On the way to this performance I was suddenly conscious of an event that I was sure would happen tonight. As the thoughts became clearer I saw the back of a playing card. Slowly it turned around until I could see the value of the card. I knew then that this card would be involved in an experiment in ESP that I had planned to conduct. I wrote down the value of the card and sealed it in an envelope. I then sealed that envelope in another and gave it to one of the spectators in our audience as he came in. Would the person holding that envelope please stand up? Thank you, sir! I'll be calling on you later. Will the person sitting next to you please come up onto the stage and assist me in the next phase of this experiment?

"Thank you, sir, for lending your support to our undertaking. Here's a deck of cards. Please shuffle it as many times as you please."

When this person is finished shuffling the cards, place the deck on the table, pick up a napkin, and spread it over one hand. Now take up the deck again and spread the napkin over the cards, saying, "I have covered the cards with this cloth. I want you to select a card from this deck of cards. To make it impossible for me to influence you in any way I want you to make this selection by cutting the deck through the cloth. That's it, grip the cards and lift them up along with the napkin. The card that you cut to is on the top of the portion of the deck that is left in my hand. Remove the top card and show it to the audience. It's the jack of hearts. Can everybody see it? Would you agree that this has been a perfectly random choice on your part? Good, I also agree. Now will the gentleman in the audience to whom I gave the envelope please stand up again? Sir, please give the envelope to anyone

**53**

around you. Very good. Now will that person kindly open the envelope, remove the sealed envelope inside it, and pass it to anyone nearby? Excellent. Now will this last person please come forward and open this final envelope and read the prediction written on the sheet inside?"

When the prediction is read it will, of course, state: "The card that will be selected during the ESP experiment tonight will be . . . the jack of hearts." Thank all of those who participated in his little experiment and acknowledge the round of applause from the audience.

## Materials needed
One deck of cards • two envelopes • a sheet of paper • a large black felt-tipped marking pen • a heavy white napkin or opaque silk handkerchief.

## Preparation
Decide what card you're going to "force" the spectator to select when he cuts the deck. Remove this card and place it on the table, *face-up*, and place the napkin over it. In the above example, the card is the jack of hearts. Take the sheet of paper and write down the name of the card in bold letters. Fold and seal this prediction in the small envelope and then seal this envelope in the larger one. Put the rest of the deck in the card case and place it on the table.

## Presentation
When your audience files in for the show, hand someone the prediction to hold. Mention that you will call on him later to assist you in one of your experiments. Caution the individual to keep the envelope out of sight until called upon.

When the spectator who is to assist you in selecting a card comes forward, remove the cards from the card case and spread then face-up, ribbon fashion, across the top of the table. Remark that although they appear to be thoroughly mixed, you want the spectator to take the deck and shuffle and cut it as many times as he pleases.

When he is finished, take the deck and, turning it face-up in your left hand, start to place it on the table in back of where the napkin is. Remember that, hidden under the napkin is the face-up jack of hearts. The spectator should be standing to your right at this time. As you start to raise the napkin with your right hand, slide the face-up deck, in your left hand, under the napkin, letting it drop down on top of the jack of hearts (Fig. 1). Practise this move until you've got

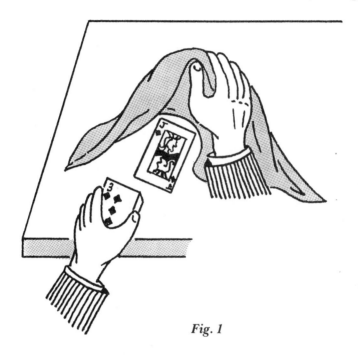

*Fig. 1*

it down pat. The napkin should hide this critical move from both the audience and from the spectator at your elbow. The action must be smooth and take only a split second to execute.

Show both sides of the napkin and retain it in your right hand. Next, reach down with your left hand and pick up the deck from the table. As you do this, turn the deck over so it is now face-down. At this point the jack of hearts is face-down on the top of the deck. Take the napkin in your right hand and drape it over your left hand. Just as the cloth is about to cover the hand, turn the deck face-up. This action is covered by the cloth.

Now request the spectator to cut the cards through the napkin. As he lifts off a portion of it, and before he pulls the napkin away from your left hand, turn the remainder of the deck in your left hand face-down. The top card of this portion of the deck is, of course, the jack of hearts. Place the deck in your left hand onto the table and instruct the spectator to turn over the top card, the one he thinks he has just cut the deck to. Just before he does this, retrieve the napkin and cards that he is holding. As he is turning the card over, reach under the napkin, turn the cards over, and bring them out, face-down.

The trick, from your point of view, is now finished. You only have to have the spectator announce the value of the card he cut to and show it to the audience.

The final bit is the rather theatrical presentation of your prediction. It is up to you to sell your audience on your uncanny abilities to foresee things that will happen in the future. Remember, a great magician is only a great actor playing the part of a magician. It can be you, if you plan well and practise hard.

# THE MASTER MENTALIST'S MEMORY DEMONSTRATION

## Effect

Every master mentalist should be able to demonstrate skill and mastery of the science of mnemonics. The following method has stood the test of time and has been used by many of the outstanding stage performers both here and abroad.

Have someone in the audience come forward to assist in this demonstration. After being blindfolded, request that the audience shout out names of various things and objects. The assistant is to write these items down on the blackboard next to the numbers 1 through 10 (Fig. 1). When ten items have been written down, state that you, still blindfolded and with your back to the board, will name the object that is associated with any number. Or, if given the object, will state the number that it is written next to.

*Fig. 1*

After doing this about a dozen times, stop the questioning and say, "Now, just to show you how infallible my memory is I'll name off all ten objects in the order given, and then I'll top that off by naming them in reverse order." Needless to say, you make good on your boast. Let's find out how!

## Materials needed

A blackboard or some other large writing surface • a blindfold.

## Preparation

None.

## Presentation

When performing this trick you really do memorize a list of 10 or 20 or more objects that are freely chosen and written on a blackboard. To accomplish this feat you must first draw up a list of objects you will then commit to memory. For the sake of illustration we have made up our own list (Fig. 2). Each number, from 1 to 10, has an object associated with it. In our case the object for number 1 is a shoe; number 2 is a black ink bottle; number 3 is a trumpet; and so on. All you have to do to remember an object called out is to associate it, in your mind, with the object that belongs to the number that it is written after. As an example; the first item called out was *car*. You know that the object associated with number 1 is a shoe. You therefore form a mental picture of a car riding down the street with a giant shoe fastened to the top of it. The more outlandish the mental picture, the easier it will be for you to remember the object.

To remember the second word, *dog*, you might think of a giant ink well tipping great black spots onto a dalmatian. This would firmly cement the word *dog* with the number 2 in your mind.

To remember the third word, *roses*, you might think of a man playing the trumpet and having *roses* coming out of it instead of notes.

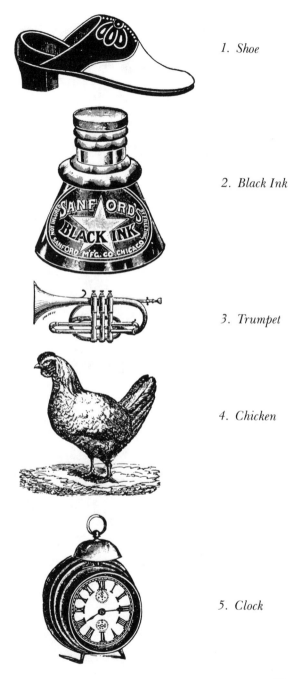

1. *Shoe*

2. *Black Ink*

3. *Trumpet*

4. *Chicken*

5. *Clock*

*Fig. 2*

6. *Parasol*

7. *False Teeth*

8. *Bell*

9. *Crab*

10. *Crown*

*Fig. 2*

With these kinds of associations it's easy to remember long lists of items. To name the selected items in order just go down your memorized number list. When you think of the shoe you'll also think of the car. The ink bottle will bring the dog to mind. The trumpet will remind you of a blast of roses. And so forth and so on.

Although there is no limit to the size of a list that you might make up and memorize, I think that the practical limit for a performance should be twenty numbers. It makes for an impressive demonstration without becoming tedious.

# Paper Magic

## THE PAPER BIRD OF JAPAN

### Effect
The magician takes a square piece of paper and transforms it, using a few simple folds, into a perfect bird that flaps its wings when its tail is pulled.

### Materials needed
One piece of stiff paper 8½″ × 11″.

### Preparation
Cut the paper into a square 8½″ × 8½″.

### Presentation
Over 70 years ago that greatest of all magicians, Harry Houdini, wrote a book on the art of paper magic. In it he revealed the secret of folding a piece of paper into the shape of a bird. I will let Mr. Houdini tell you how it's done.

"In the days before the cabaret, New York boasted a considerable number of popular dining clubs which brought together a host of people who could 'do entertaining things.' At one of these dinners I observed a Japanese gentleman folding a leaf of the menu card in a peculiar manner. Gradually all those within 'seeing distance' became interested, and before he finished he was quite surrounded by spectators who applauded him roundly when, from that scrap of pasteboard, he at last produced a little paper bird that flapped its wings quite naturally.

"Since then the clever gentleman has taught me how to make the bird. Here is the trick: Take a square piece of letter paper six inches or more in size and fold from corner to corner in each direction and then across the center both ways, making all the folds sharp in order that they may serve as guides in the further folding. The sheet will then appear as in Fig. 1. Now fold the side $a$, $h$, $g$, over to the line $a$, $e$, as in

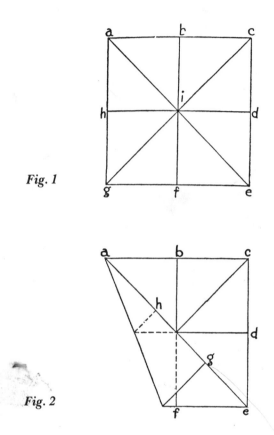

Fig. 1

Fig. 2

Fig. 2, and sharpen the fold from $a$ to $h$ *only*, merely bending the remainder of the fold. Fold the side $a$, $b$, $c$, to the line $a$, $e$, and sharpen the line from $a$ to $b$ only. Repeat this with the remaining three corners, and you will then find that you have a dish-shaped, four-cornered star, as in Fig. 3, the heavy lines showing the edge of the paper. Fold this star upward on line $h$, $d$, with the sides doubled inward and you will have Fig. 4. Holding this with the thumb and fingers of both hands at

**63**

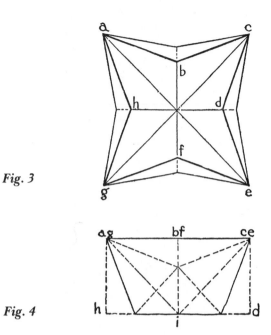

*Fig. 3*

*Fig. 4*

the points marked *e* and *g*, bring the hands together, being sure that the points *b*, *f*, *h*, and *d* fold inward and downward, and the result will be Fig. 5. After this, fold the point *c*

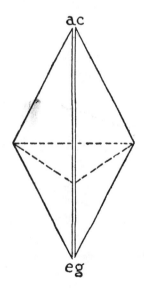

*Fig. 5*

downward toward your body and the point *a* downward in the opposite direction, thus forming Fig. 6, and then open

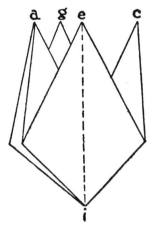

**Fig. 6**

the fold and double downward to the right and the same to the left. Turn the paper with the points to the top and you form Fig. 7. Pull point *g* down to the right to form the tail and

**Fig. 7**

press the new folds thus made, then point *e* down to the left not quite so far, forming the neck. To make the head, open the fold at *e* and bend the head at right angles to the neck; by pressing the folds together again the head will take just the proper angle, as shown in Fig. 8. Crush down the sharp point

*Fig. 8*

between the wings *a* and *c*, and blow in the little hole below the wings, which will inflate the body. The wings should be bent outward a little as shown. By holding the bird with the thumb and finger as the point marked *o*, and pulling the tail with the other hand, the wings can be made to flap (Fig. 9)."

Over the span of 70 years that explanation still comes in loud and clear. Thank you, Mr. Harry Houdini.

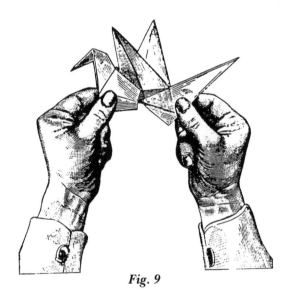

*Fig. 9*

# THE PUZZLING PAPER PUFF BALL

## Effect

The following item is both a puzzle and a game I'm sure you will find use for. It is a paper ball that, once put together, can be handed out with the following challenge: Take apart this ball and put it back together again without ripping the paper parts.

This is a very difficult puzzle. It should be constructed of light cardboard. Cut out three circles, each 3 inches in diameter (Figs. 1, 2, and 4). Slits must then be cut in each circle as indicated by the dotted lines. Fold the two sides marked A, A, in Fig. 1 and pass the upper half of Fig. 1

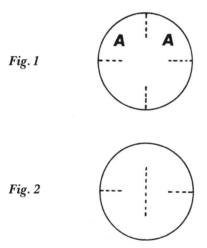

*Fig. 1*

*Fig. 2*

through the center slit in Fig. 2. Open up Fig. 1 and you will have a construction like that in Fig. 3. Now, fold the four

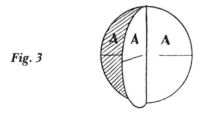

*Fig. 3*

upper halves marked *A, A, A, A* (Fig. 3) together and pass through the star slit in Fig. 4. When it is halfway through, open up the folds and you will have Fig. 5, a paper puff ball.

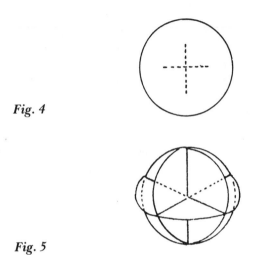

*Fig. 4*

*Fig. 5*

An amusing game is played using several of these paper balls. Mark each with a number and give contestants paper straws. Line the puff balls up along one side of a table and have a race, seeing which player can force his puff ball along first to the opposite end of the table by blowing through the straw. Children will find these puff balls a lot of fun to throw around, and they are not likely to injure anyone.

# TINTINNABULATION

## Effect

"Ladies and gentlemen, this is certainly one of the finest tintinnabulating puzzles I have ever seen. Step a little closer, please, so you can examine the paper puzzle that I am holding in my hand [Fig. 1]. It is constructed of three fairly

**Fig. 1**

stiff pieces of paper. The puzzle, ladies and gentlemen, is to discover just how they were put together without tearing or mutilating any of the fragile pieces. Please note that the paper bell is firmly locked onto the large paper link by the smaller paper link. The hole in the small link, however, is far too small for either side of the bell to pass through it. How was it done? A ringing solution from one of you is needed. Now, who would like to try it first?"

## Materials needed

A sheet of heavy paper • a pair of scissors.

## Preparation

Cut out the three puzzle pieces shown in Figures 2, 3, and 4. Bend, but do not crease, the large link (b), in Figure 5, and slip the small link over the end marked (d). Now, hang the bell on the link as shown in Figure 5 and slip the small link back over end (d) and down onto the bell. Open up the large

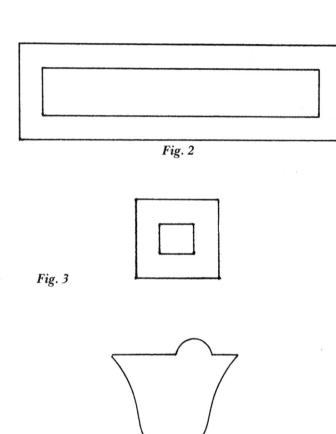

*Fig. 2*

*Fig. 3*

*Fig. 4*

link and the puzzle is completed (Fig. 6). Because you bent the large link but did not crease it, there will be no indication that it was ever folded.

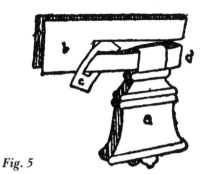

*Fig. 5*

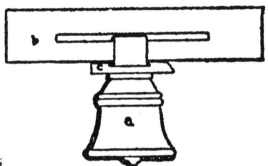

*Fig. 6*

## Presentation

There is little more to be said about this interesting little paper item. To take the puzzle apart merely reverse the steps for assembling it that were given in the Preparation section above. Your friends will rack their brains trying to solve this one.

# Rope Magic

## THE GREAT CUT-AND-RESTORED ROPE TRICK

### Effect

One of the basic tricks magicians love is the restoration of some article that has been torn or cut up into many pieces. They are always putting playing cards or pieces of colored paper back together. Here is a quick and astonishing feat along these lines employing a piece of rope and a pair of scissors.

Take a length of rope and after finding the center of it, cut it cleanly in two with the scissors. Then tie the two pieces together, wrap the rope around one hand, touch the rope with your magic wand and, presto-chango, the rope is once again whole and unblemished. Immediately hand it out for examination.

### Materials needed

One piece of soft rope around four feet in length • a pair of scissor • a wand • a prop box.

### Preparation

A prop box is a small, decorated box that can hold cards, silks, rope, scissors, and other items that will be used during your act. We'll discuss the makeup of this box at the end of this presentation.

### Presentation

First, remove a four-foot length of rope from your prop box and hold it up in your left hand (Fig. 1). State that for your next trick you will need two pieces of rope of exactly the

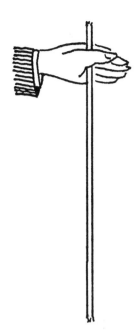

*Fig. 1*

same length. Drop your right hand down in back of the rope and catch a loop of it on the back of your hand. Lift it up and move your right hand towards your left hand (Fig. 2). Note that at all times the back of your left hand will be towards the audience. This will mask the following critical moves from their sight.

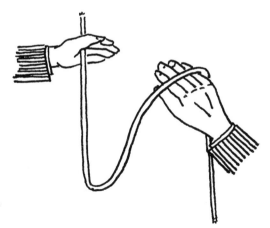

*Fig. 2*

When the fingers of your right hand reach the palm of your left hand, the first two fingers clip the rope a couple of inches below your left thumb. At this moment you also tilt the right hand upwards so that the loop of rope on the back of the hand slides forward (Fig. 3). The two fingers of the right

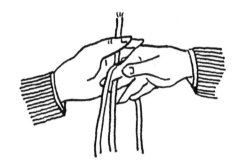

**Fig. 3**

hand now pull the clipped portion of the rope upwards a couple of inches above the left hand (Fig. 4). The left thumb

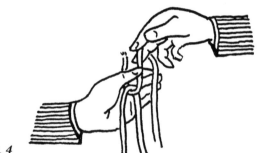

**Fig. 4**

and forefinger now move together to hold the newly formed loop "A" (Fig. 5). The right hand now picks up the scissors and cuts the rope at point "A."

In Figure 6 we see how the situation looks from your point of view. You now pretend to tie the two pieces of rope together (Fig. 7). What you are really doing is tying the three-inch piece of rope around the larger piece with a single knot. Now take hold of one end of the rope with your left hand and

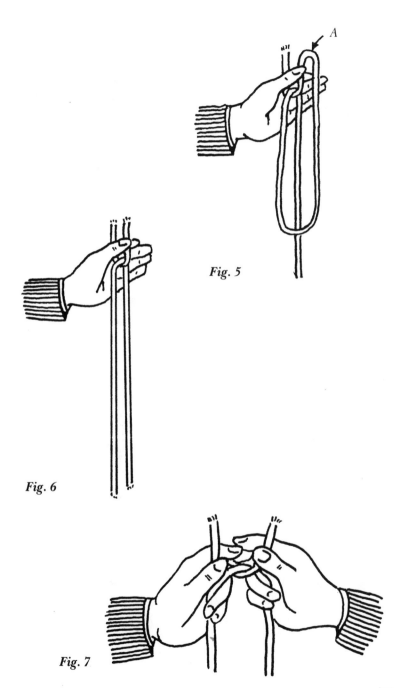

*A*

*Fig. 5*

*Fig. 6*

*Fig. 7*

let it hang down. At this point look at the rope and state that you've made a mistake and that your next trick really calls for the use of a single piece of rope. However, since you're a magician this should be no problem at all since all you have to do is to make the rope whole once again. Proceed to wrap the rope up around your left hand. As you wrap the rope around your left hand it passes through your closed right hand. When the small fake knot reaches your right palm you take hold of it. The remainder of the rope now slides easily through this knot while being wrapped around your left hand. When the rope is completely wrapped around your left hand, your closed right hand, containing the knot, moves over to the table to pick up the magic wand which is perched on top of the prop box (Fig. 8). As your hand

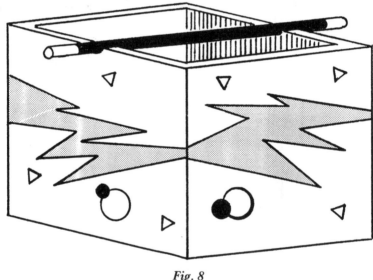

**Fig. 8**

reaches the wand you open your fingers and let the knot drop into the box. This action is screened from the audience by the back of your hand and the front of the box. All during this action, hold your left hand high so that the audience does not lose sight of it for a moment. This way you can't be accused of switching the rope. Pick up the wand and tap it against the rope and state that it is whole once again. You then tilt your hand downwards and let the rope uncoil itself so everyone can see that it has indeed been miraculously restored to its former state.

## Notes

The prop box mentioned above is quite simple to make. Constructed of plywood, it measures twelve inches on all sides, thus forming an open cube (Fig. 8). There is no top to the box. Paint all sides of the box, inside and out, with a primer coat of white paint and then decorate it, using oil-based paint for durability, to suit your style. Note the two half-circle notches cut into the edges of the two side panels. These keep the wand from rolling about when you place it across the top of the box prior to the presentation of the above rope trick.

Besides being a convenient place to dispose of secreted items, the box is a perfect receptacle for holding your props while performing.

# HOW TO STRETCH A PIECE
## OF ROPE

## Effect

Walk onto the stage carrying three pieces of rope. Start to do a trick and suddenly notice that two of the pieces are of the same length. Explain to the audience that you should have three pieces, each of a different length, to perform this opening trick. "Well, I guess that I'll just have to use a rope stretcher and fix one of these pieces. Does anyone out there happen to have one? No! Well I guess I'll just have to do it the hard way!"

So saying, place two of the pieces aside on a table. Then grasp hold of both ends of the rope and proceed to stretch it until it's fully six or seven times its original length. Exclaim: "I seem to have gotten carried away with this rope-stretching business," Take up a pair of scissors and say, "If I trim off eight and a half feet I'll have the piece I need for my opening number." Suiting your actions to your words, cut off the required piece, pick up the two shorter pieces that you put aside, and launch into your presentation of "The Impossible Rope Trick" (You'll find a complete description of this trick in my book *World's Best Magic Tricks*).

## Materials needed

One piece of soft rope twelve feet long • one piece twenty-eight inches long • one piece twelve inches long • a pair of scissors.

## Preparation

Double up the twelve-foot length of rope and take the two ends in your right hand. While holding on tightly to the rope put on your jacket. With your jacket on, place one end of the rope over your right first finger and pull it down twelve inches. Take the other end of the rope and place it over, and under, your little finger. Pull on it until it hangs down twelve inches. Now, take the rest of the rope, the part that is hanging out of your inside sleeve, fold it up, and tuck it into the right-inside pocket of your jacket (Fig. 1).

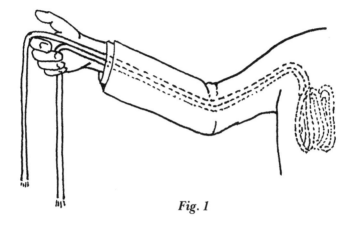

*Fig. 1*

Take the twenty-eight-inch piece of rope and drape it over your right hand so the ends match the ends of the rope that you just positioned in that hand. It will look as though you are holding two pieces of rope that are of the same length. Finally, drape the twelve-inch piece of rope over these two pieces and you are ready to present the trick.

## Presentation

Enter stage-left with the back of your right hand towards the audience and the palm side against your right side, waist high. As you reach the table look at the ropes and pretend to discover that one of them is the wrong length. You then place the twelve-inch and the twenty-eight-inch pieces of rope on the table. Explain that the only way you can present your first trick is by stretching the rope in your right hand. Take hold of the end that is draped over your right forefinger with your left hand and start pulling on the rope with your *right hand*. At least this is what you appear to be doing. Actually, as you make the pulling motion, left to right, with your right hand, you are actually letting the rope, concealed in your right

**79**

arm, slide out through your thumb and forefinger. It's important that your left hand remain in a fixed position while your right hand moves away and slightly downwards. This gives the "illusion" that the right hand is actually stretching the rope (Fig. 2).

*Fig. 2*

After pulling around two feet of rope out of your sleeve, let go of the rope in your left hand. Your right hand then moves back up to the left hand. Take hold of the rope again with your left hand, at the point where the rope comes out of your right hand (Fig. 3). Repeat the stretching maneuver described above. Keep doing this until the entire rope has been pulled out of your jacket.

One thing you must remember: Never pull with the left hand. To do so would immediately make it apparent that you were pulling the rope out of your right sleeve. Done the correct way, the illusion is perfect. You don't necessarily have

**Fig. 3**

to present this trick using the two other pieces of rope. Their inclusion helps create the idea in the minds of your audience that you have entered carrying three pieces of rope. Also, their inclusion provides a logical segue into "The Impossible Rope Trick." You can, of course, discard the two other pieces of rope and come up with some other pretext for the need to stretch the rope in your hand.

# Money Magic

## AN INFLATIONARY LESSON

### Effect

In this trick you remove two folded bills from your pocket and hold them up for all to see (see Fig. 1). Mention how, many years ago, your father had put them aside for a rainy day. The funny thing about these bills, however, is that while forty years ago they were really worth something, today their value has decreased by fifty percent. To illustrate this point, unfold the bills and place them on the table. In the process one of the bills instantly disappears.

*Fig. 1*

### Materials

One crisp new bill of your choice.

## Preparation

Place the bill on the table in front of you, face-up. Turn the bill over and fold it lengthwise along line *a-a*. Crease the bill and open it. Repeat this action, creasing the bill along the center-width line *b-b* (see Fig. 2). With the bill still folded take

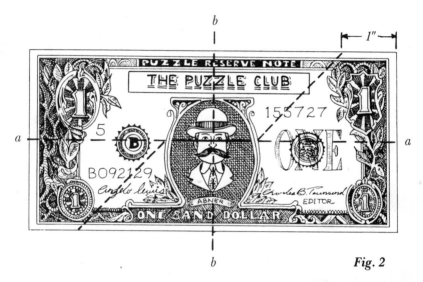

*Fig. 2*

a razor blade and make a slit along the center line from the edge of the portrait frame to the edge of the bill as indicated by the arrow in Figure 3.

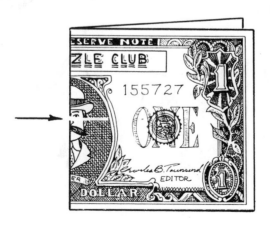

*Fig. 3*

Now for the last two folds. Open out the bill once more and fold it along the long edge *a-a*. Now fold the right side of the bill up behind the bill along the dash-line, as shown in Figure 2. Crease the edge and do the same on the left side of the bill, folding the bill down and under along a line going from the edge of the portrait to a point one inch from the left bottom corner of the bill. Crease this fold and open the bill up.

For the last time, fold the bill along line *a-a*. Take hold of the two opposite ends of the bill with the thumb and first finger of each hand, and bring your hands together, causing the bill to open up in the center at the slit you made in it. The bill should now be taking on the appearance of two folded bills, one sitting on top of the other as they appear in Figure 1. Press down all the creases and you're ready to present this minute mystery.

## Presentation

Remove the folded bill from your pocket, holding it as shown in Figure 1. Show it all around, turning it over so that your audience can see both sides of the gimmicked bill. As you come to the end of your reference to the powers of inflation, take hold of both ends of the bill and smartly pull them apart, giving the illusion of two bills suddenly turned into one. Holding the bill tightly so that the slit doesn't open up, spread it out on the table. Carefully turn it over so that all can see that there is only one bill there. You can even pick it up with one hand, placing your fingers over the center of the bill on the back and your thumb covering the front center. Once again, show the bill back and front, fold it up, replace it in your pocket, and quickly move on to your next mystery, leaving your audience with something to ponder about at their leisure.

# THE BIG MONEY GIVEAWAY TRICK

## Effect

State that you're in a generous mood tonight and so you're going to try and give away some money. Hold up five sealed envelopes and say that one of them contains paper money while the others contain only "pearls of wisdom." Have four people come forward to assist in the distribution of this largess. Hand the envelopes to one of them to mix up before the distribution. When they have been thoroughly shuffled, take them back and hand them to one of the other spectators.

Instruct the person to shift one envelope from the top of the stack to the bottom of the stack while spelling out the word "money," and with each letter to shift one envelope from the top of the stack to the bottom. Tell the person that at the letter "Y" he should keep that envelope and pass the rest to the next person in line. That individual, in turn, is to do the same, keeping the envelope when the letter "Y" comes up. After the third and fourth spectators do likewise, the last envelope is passed back to you.

"All right," you now say, "everyone open his envelope and we'll see who the big winner is!" Needless to say, you always end up with the money. The others get to keep the "pearls of wisdom" as souvenirs of the night's entertainment.

## Materials needed

One crisp new bill • five heavy plain envelopes • four pieces of paper with the "pearls of wisdom" written on them.

## Preparation

Seal the bill in one of the envelopes. Mark the envelope with a small dot in the lower left-hand corner (Fig. 1). Write your messages on the four slips of paper and seal them in the other envelopes. Suggested "pearls of wisdom" are:

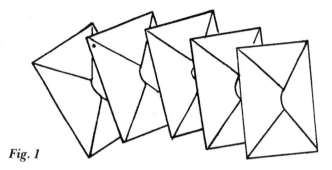

*Fig. 1*

"I have never let my schooling interfere with my education."—Mark Twain

"If you think education is expensive, try ignorance."—Derek Bok

"Have children while your parents are still young enough to take care of them."—Rita Rudner

"Hard work never killed anybody, but why take a chance?"—Charlie McCarthy

## Presentation

Once again, a performer's delight: a trick that practically works itself. After the spectator has mixed the envelopes and handed them back to you, pretend to give them an added shuffle while the remaining three spectators come forward from the audience. However, what you are really doing is looking for the envelope which contains the money (the envelope with the dot on it) and intending to position it so it is second from the top of the pack. Once this has been done, pass the stack of envelopes to the first spectator and let the "spelling bee" begin.

The rest is automatic. Have each person read out the quotation on his slip before you thank the participants for their help and send them back to their seats.

# THE IMPOSSIBLE COIN VANISH

## Effect

State that you will attempt to make a coin vanish under impossible test conditions. Request three spectators to come forward to assist you. After removing your coat and rolling up your right sleeve, ask for the loan of a large-size coin. Hold your right arm out with the coin in your fingertips (Fig. 1). Then throw a large silk cloth, or handkerchief, over your hand (Fig. 2). Ask each spectator one by one to reach

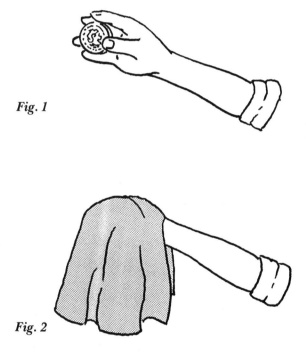

*Fig. 1*

*Fig. 2*

under the silk and feel that the coin is still there. Then count to three and state that the coin has now vanished. Have one of the spectators remove the silk, revealing that the coin has indeed vanished from your hand. The silk also proves to be empty. At all times your hand is away from your body. State that unfortunately the person who taught you this trick neglected to show you how to get the coin back. Reach into your own pocket, remove the amount of money you borrowed, and give it to the person you borrowed it from, saying, "I always lose money when I perform this little miracle!"

## Materials needed
A piece of heavy silk or a handkerchief • a borrowed coin.

## Preparation
None.

## Presentation
This trick is very easy to do. All you need is a confederate in the audience. When you pick the three members of the audience to assist you, make sure that your confederate is one of them. When your hand is covered by the silk and the spectators reach under to feel the coin, you make sure that your confederate is the last one to check on the coin. Under cover of the silk, he takes the coin from your fingers and palms it in his own hand. He states that the coin is still there and drops his hand to his side. As he does this, turn and extend your covered hand towards the audience. All eyes will follow your hand. Count to three and state that the coin is gone. As you say this, extend your hand towards the first spectator who reached under the silk and instruct him to remove it. While the spectator is doing this the confederate can momentarily place his hand into his own pocket and get rid of the coin. When the silk is removed all that is visible is the performer's bare arm and hand.

Confederates are seldom used in magic. Since magic is an art form, one can't help but feel that their use is akin to cheating. However, on occasion, and under the right circumstances, a truly impossible feat can be pulled off, such as the vanishing coin described here. Give this one a try and see how it works for you.

# Card Magic

## THE RED-AND-BLACK-CARD MYSTERY

### Effect

Shuffle a deck of cards and then spread the cards face-up on the table so everyone can see how thoroughly they have been mixed. Then gather up the cards and deal them into two equal piles. When the piles are turned face-up and spread across the table, show your audience that all the red cards have migrated to one pile and all the black cards to the other.

### Materials

One deck of cards.

### Preparation

Take the deck and divide it into piles, one containing all the red cards and the other containing all the black ones. Now, arrange them into one pile, face-up, alternating the colors red, black, red, black, etc. When you're done, place the deck back in its card case. You are now ready to present the trick.

### Presentation

Take the card case from your pocket and remove the deck. Explain to your audience that you are going to show them a feat with cards that is off the beaten path. Cut the deck a few times and give it a riffle shuffle, making sure the cards are well mixed. Do not shuffle them more than once. Next, take the deck, turn it face-up, and spread the cards across the table. Everyone can now see how thoroughly the cards are mixed. While you let your audience look at the cards for a few seconds, scan the cards until you find two cards of the same color next to one another. When you find such a pair, preferably near the center of the spread, reach down and separate the pair, picking up the section of the deck to the right of the pair. Place these cards, face-up, in your right hand. With your left hand scoop up the remaining cards and place them face-up on top of the cards in your right hand. In effect, what you have done is to cut the deck and place the top half under the bottom half.

Turn the deck face-down and state that you are now going to divide the cards into two equal piles. Deal the cards face-down onto the table into two piles, alternating the cards being dealt, first to one pile and then the other, until you have twenty-six cards in each. At this point have one of the spectators select one pile and take it into his hands. You say:

"I want you to turn the cards over slowly, one at a time, and place them into two piles on the table. All the red cards go into one pile on your left and all the black cards into another on your right. At the same time, I will deal one card face-down from my stack into two piles diagonally opposite to your piles. When we're finished dealing out the cards, I promise you, a startling thing will have taken place." Figure 1 shows how the cards are dealt onto the table.

Spectator's Piles

Black cards                    Red cards

When a red card is dealt, place your next card on this pile

When a black card is dealt, place your next card on this pile

**Fig. 1**                    Magician's Piles

When the cards are all back on the table, turn the cards in the spectator's two piles face-down. Next, place each of these piles on top of the two directly opposite to them. (See Figure 2.)

*Black cards*                    *Red cards*

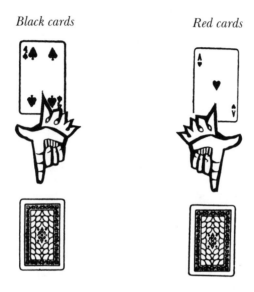

**Fig. 2**

"In the beginning we cut the deck several times. We then shuffled the cards together until they were well mixed. We divided them into two decks and then divided them again into four. And yet, like oil and water, the red cards insisted on coming together in one pack and the black cards into the other."

As you say this, spread the cards in each pack face-up on the table. If you followed the above instructions faithfully the trick works itself. Practise this one well and you will have a mystifying feat to start any card routine with.

# A DEVILISH GAME OF POKER

## Effect

Here's a neat poker setup that works itself. Remove a deck of cards from its case and give it a few shuffles and cuts while remarking on how hard it is to get a good poker hand when you really need one. To illustrate, deal out five hands of poker onto the table. Turn them all over and point out that not one hand is higher than a pair of sixes, which isn't even good enough to open the pot.

Gather up the five hands and place them back on top of the deck. "The funny thing about cards is that after dealing out five rotten hands you can turn around and deal out these same cards and come up with some surprising results." You once again deal out five hands on the table using the same twenty-five cards you have just placed on the top of the deck.

"Let's say we're playing a game of showdown poker, where everyone gets only five cards and the high hand wins. How many of these hands do you think would be good enough to stay in the betting?" Turning over the first hand, you say, "This gent has a five-card straight, so he'll open the betting. This next hand contains a five-card flush, which would rate a hefty raise. Oh, oh, what do we have here! The third hand contains a full house, which is good for a second raise. Whoa! Look at the fourth hand! It contains four aces. That should be good for the pot! But wait, would you believe it? The dealer has a straight flush! In the Old West the lead would be flying after a deal like that!"

## Materials needed

One prepared deck of playing cards.

## Preparation

Take the deck and, from left to right, lay out the following five hands:

A straight, using 3♣, 4♦, 5♠, 6♥, 7♦;
a flush, using 2♠, 4♠, 6♠, 7♠, 8♠;
a full house, using 5♣, 5♦, 5♥, 3♠, 3♥;
four of a kind, using A♥, A♠, A♣, A♦, 8♥;
a straight flush, using K♦, Q♦, J♦, 10♦, 9♦.

Now, starting with the hand containing the straight flush (hand five), place hand four on top of hand five; place hand three on top of hand four; hand two on hand three; and finally hand one on hand two. Now, turn these twenty-five cards face-down and place them on top of the remaining cards of the deck. Place the complete deck back in its case and you're ready to go.

## Presentation

This card trick practically works itself, provided you deal the cards face-down both times. This is crucial. Remove the deck from the case and give it a couple of false shuffles while making your remarks about poker hands. Just make sure that the top twenty-five cards are left undisturbed while you're doing this. When you deal out the first five hands, the highest one will contain a pair of eights. When you gather up the cards prior to the second deal, stack the hands face-up, in any order. Just don't mix any cards from one hand with any of the cards from another. When you've stacked the five hands, turn them face-down and add them to the top of the remaining cards. When you deal them out this time, the hands will fall, left to right, just as described in the first section of this presentation. This is really a very nice bit of poker fun.

# ANOTHER POKER DEAL SETUP

## Effect

In this poker routine, after shuffling and cutting the deck you deal out two poker hands, one for the spectator and one for yourself. Deal the cards face-up onto the table. The spectator is dealt a straight, ten to ace, but loses to the performer, who has a full house, aces over kings.

Gather up the cards, saying, "The first hand is mine. I'll give you another chance to win your money back." Once again, deal two hands face-up. This time the spectator has three kings. However, you come up with four aces. "So far, your luck is all bad," you comment. "I'll give you one more chance! Double or nothing!"

For the last time, gather up the cards and deal out two hands face-down. "All right, let's see if you have finally beaten me." Turning over the spectator's cards, you exclaim, "This time you have the full house, aces over kings. It will take a miracle to beat that hand! Speaking of miracles, look what I've got! A royal straight flush! I guess luck is on my side today!"

Don't you believe it. Here's how it's done.

## Materials needed

One prepared deck of cards.

## Preparation

The setup needed to effect this delightful pasteboard interlude was invented by the late Dai Vernon, one of the giants of modern magic. Remove the following ten cards and place them on top of the deck in the following order, from the top down:

10♠, A♥, A♦, K♥, K♦, A♠, J♠, K♠, Q♠, A♣

The 10♠ is now face-down on top of the deck.

Place the deck back in its card case and you're ready to go.

# Presentation

Remove the cards from the case and shuffle the deck a few times. When doing this, make sure that the top ten cards are left undisturbed. Next, execute one or two false cuts. Start by dealing two hands face-up onto the table. Place the deck aside. When dealing the hands, place each succeeding card on top of the previous card in an overlapping fashion. When you have finished dealing, each hand should have the appearance of a fan.

You win the first hand with a full house over a straight. Close up each of the hands and turn them face-down on the table. Place the *spectator's cards on top of your cards*, pick up the stack, and deal the second round of poker hands face-up. Once again, make sure the cards overlap each other in a fan-like fashion.

This time your four aces beat out the spectator's three kings. For the last time, square up the hands and turn them face-down. Place *your cards on top of the spectator's cards* and deal out the final two hands. When the two hands are turned over, triumph for the third time, now with a royal straight flush!

# THE UNDER-AND-UP CARD MYSTERY

## Effect

The following brief item is merely a prelude to more serious card work. Removing the playing cards from their case, deal thirteen cards into a small pile on the table. Placing the rest of the deck aside, pick the stack up and turn it over. Fanning them across the table, remark, "I have here thirteen well-mixed cards." Square the deck up and turn it face-down, saying, "A very odd thing has been happening to me lately. If I tap a deck of cards three times with my fist and then deal them out in an under-and-up fashion, a most surprising thing happens. The cards come out in ascending order, ace through king. Watch!" Take the top card and place it under the packet and then turn the next card face-up. This turns out to be an ace, which you place on the table. Take the next top card and place it under the deck and turn the next card face-up. This card is a two. Place it with the ace on the table. Continue along in this fashion until all of the cards are face-up on the table in ascending order, ace through king.

## Materials

One deck of playing cards.

## Preparation

Arrange the top thirteen cards of the deck as follows: 10, 6, king, 5, 9, 4, jack, 3, 8, 2, queen, ace, 7. Mix the suits so that when the cards are fanned they present a random picture.

## Presentation

Take the deck from the case and give it a few false cuts while talking about card magic in general. After a moment or two deal the top thirteen cards, one at a time, down onto the table to form a small pile. This effectively reverses the original setup. The cards are now arranged, from the top of the pile down: 7, ace, queen, 2, 8, 3, jack, 4, 9, 5, king, 6, and 10. From this point on the trick works itself. Place the top card under the pack and turn up the next one and place it on the table. Continue in this manner until all of the cards are face-up on the table.

This problem can also be presented as a puzzle where the audience is challenged to try and figure out how you originally set up the deck so the cards would come out in ascending order, ace through king. They'll soon find out that this is far from being an easy problem to solve.

# THE THREE-CARD MONTE TRICK

## Effect

The three-card monte trick is as old as the hills. The following description of it was written over one hundred years ago by that famous author Professor Hoffmann. The amazing thing about this trick, or should I say swindle, is that its basic presentation hasn't changed much in all of that time. While strolling on Fifth Avenue in New York City I've witnessed many demonstrations of this game that followed, in every detail, the methods illustrated in Professor Hoffmann's description. Let's hear what the good professor had to say about it.

"Good afternoon, my friends. It's so good to see you all here and having such a fine time. My first trick is called the three-card trick. This is more of a sharper's than a conjurer's trick, but it is a frequent experience with anyone who is known to dabble in sleight-of-hand to be asked, 'Can you do a three-card trick?' It is humiliating to be obliged to reply, 'No, I can't,' and moreover the trick, when neatly performed, may be made the occasion of a good deal of fun.

"The effect of the trick is as follows: Three cards are used, one of them being a court card, the two others plain or low cards. We will suppose, for the sake of illustration, that the cards used are the king of hearts, the seven of spades, and the nine of diamonds. The performer takes one of the low cards, say the nine of diamonds, in his left hand face-down, between the tips of the second finger and thumb. The other two cards are held in the right hand in like manner one above the other, about an inch apart; but the uppermost card, which we will suppose to be the seven, is held between the thumb and the tip of the first finger, while the undermost (the king) is supported between the thumb and the second finger [see Fig. 1]. The performer now throws the three cards in succession face-down upon a table or on the ground before him (in the latter case kneeling to do his

**Fig. 1**

work), shuffles them about with more or less rapidity, and then invites the spectators to guess (or, in the cardsharping form of the trick, to bet) which is the court card. This would seem to be a perfectly easy matter. The spectators have observed where the king originally fell; and the subsequent shifting of the cards has not made it much more difficult to keep note of its position, but if the trick has been skillfully performed they will be much more often wrong than right.

"The main secret lies in the position of the cards in the right hand, coupled with a dexterity acquired by much practice. The performer professedly throws down the *undermost* of the two cards in the right hand first, and this card has been seen to be the king. As a matter of fact, however, he can at pleasure let the uppermost card fall first, the first finger, which supported it, taking the place of the middle finger at the top of the second card. The change is so subtle that even the keenest eye cannot detect whether it has or has not been made, and this makes practically two chances to one against the person guessing.

"This would seem to be pretty good odds, but they are not enough for the cardsharper, and in the swindling form of the trick as practiced on racecourses, etc., a new deception is introduced. The player works in conjunction with two or three confederates, each suitably disguised; say as a parson, a farmer, or a country yokel. These gentlemen start the betting, and, as might be expected, pick out the right card each time, the performer at the outset making no attempt to disguise its identity. Presently one of them takes an opportunity, while the performer's attention is professedly taken up in pushing back bystanders who are crowding him, or the like, to turn up the king, show it to the company, and in replacing it slightly to bend up one corner. The operator, a good innocent man, takes up the cards again, little thinking (of course) of the trick that has been played him, and begins to shuffle them about once more. Move them as he will, that telltale corner marks the king, and presently some bystander, whose greed is greater than his honesty, ventures a bet that he will pick out the card. Others follow the example, only too glad to bet on a supposed certainty, and not deeply concerned with the morality of the proceeding. When no more bets are to be procured, one of the victims turns up the supposed king, and finds instead the seven of spades, the fact being that the performer, in throwing down the cards for the last time, had with the point of the finger deftly straightened the bent corner of the king, and made a corresponding dog's ear on the low card.

"The moral of this little apologue is obvious. Don't try to take a mean advantage of a poor cardsharper, and if you don't want *him* to take advantage of *you, don't bet on the three-card trick,* or any other."

As I mentioned earlier, I've seen three-card monte being played on Fifth Avenue just as described by Professor Hoffmann, right down to the use of three or four shills pretending to play the game while waiting to rope in a mark. However, instead of dressing up as farmers or parsons they were usually attired in business suits and carried attaché cases. Thanks for the good advice, Professor.

# A CLEVER COINCIDENCE?

## Effect

Have a spectator shuffle a deck of cards several times and then hand it to you. Then state that you need two assistants to help you with your next trick. You will, however, get them from the pack instead of the audience. Fan the deck and, after looking over the faces for a moment or two, remove two of the cards and place them to the side, face-up. Let us say that the cards removed are the jack of clubs and the four of hearts.

Then square up the deck and hand it to the person who previously shuffled it. "I want you to take this deck and deal the cards one by one, face-down, into a pile on the table. You can deal any number of cards you want. . . . Are you sure that's enough? You can add another card if you want. No. . . . All right, take this jack of clubs that I removed from the deck, put it face-up on top of the cards on the table, and place the rest of the cards in your hand on top of the pile.

"Now, let's do it again. Pick up the deck and start dealing the cards out, one by one, into a pile on the table. Stop any time you want. You're sure that's enough? Do you want to take back that last card? No? Okay, drop the four of hearts face-up on top of the pile and then drop the rest of the deck on top of that.

"And now, folks, it's time to explain what this trick is all about. I've kept you in the dark so there could be no chance of any chicanery. What we're dealing with is an experiment in 'coincidence.' Let's see what happened. Please spread the deck out, ribbon fashion, across the top of the table. Note that there are two cards face-up among the cards, the same two cards, the jack of clubs and the four of hearts, that I had you place into the deck to mark where you stopped dealing. Please remove the jack of clubs and the next card above it and place them to the left. Now, remove the four of hearts and the next card above it and place them to the right. Wouldn't it be interesting if the card next to the jack of clubs turned out to be it's twin, the jack of spades? Let's turn it over and find out! Yes, it is! Now isn't that a coincidence?

"Do you think that this could happen a second time? Could some unknown force have guided your thoughts to have stopped not once but twice at a kindred card? Turn over the card next to the four of hearts and find out! Well, bless my soul, it's the four of diamonds. A second set of twins has been delivered. I don't know how you did it, but you have certainly given us an excellent example of 'coincidental card conjuring.' Please don't tell anyone how you did it!"

## Materials
One deck of cards.

## Preparation
None.

## Presentation
You can perform this interesting feat at the drop of a hat without the slightest bit of preparation. The secret lies in your selection of the two cards you chose from the pack to act as your "assistants." When you pick up the deck and fan it in front of you, note what card is on the top of the pack and what card is on the bottom. In our example the top card is the four of diamonds. You quickly scan the rest of the deck until you find the "twin" of this card, the four of hearts, and remove it from the deck. Next, note the bottom card, which was the jack of spades, look for its twin, the jack of clubs, and remove that card from the deck.

The trick, as far as you are concerned, is done. Square up the deck and hand it to the spectator who is to assist you. When the spectator deals the top card face-down to form a pile, this will put the four of diamonds on the bottom. The spectator can now deal as many cards as he wishes onto the pile. When he stops, have him drop the jack of clubs face-up on top of the pile and the rest of the cards in his hand on top of that. Since the bottom card of the deck in your hand is the jack of spades, the two "twin" jacks are now together.

The same holds true when you deal the second pile. The one thing you must make sure of, though, is that the spectator stops dealing to the pile before reaching the face-up card. If the spectator gets close to it, tell him it's time to stop dealing. When he stops dealing, place the four of hearts face-up on the pile and have him place the remaining cards in his hand on top. The bottom card of this portion of the deck is the four of diamonds, as was pointed out earlier. We now have the second set of "twins" together.

All that is left is for you to explain what this experiment was all about and to show the results of this little bit of "coincidental card conjuring." Emphasize that at all times the cards were in the hands of the spectator, and that it was he who made the fateful decisions as to when the building of each pile was to cease.

# THE TRAVELLING CARDS

## Effect

While idly shuffling a deck of cards, comment on how it's possible to make cards travel around in a deck, and eventually come together, merely by cutting the deck a few times. To demonstrate this phenomenon place the deck on the table and request the spectator to cut it and place the top portion in front of himself and the bottom portion in front of you. You and the spectator now each select a card from your respective halves of the deck. After making the selection, you each place this card on the top of the half of the deck it came from (he on his, you on yours). Now place your half of the deck on top of the spectator's and remark, "We have each selected a card from the deck. Your card is in the middle and my card is on top. I want you to cut the deck several times. When you're finished I will cause the two cards to travel around in the deck until they finally come together. Start cutting!"

After the spectator has cut the deck three or four times, you say, "The card I selected was the king of diamonds. What was your card?" In answer let's say the spectator responds, "My card was the three of hearts." Rap the deck three times and say, "Cards, I command you to come together in the deck!" Tell the spectator to turn the deck over, fan it out, and search for his card. Sure enough, when he finds it, yours will be next to it. An interesting journey, indeed.

## Materials needed

A deck of cards.

## Preparation

None.

## Presentation

In the beginning of the trick when you're shuffling the deck and talking about "travelling" cards, catch a glimpse of the bottom card. In the example described above, that card was the king of diamonds. After the spectator cuts the cards, he gives you the bottom half of the deck, the one with the king of diamonds on the bottom. When you select a card from your half of the deck you only pretend to memorize it before placing it on top of your pile. After he places his selected card on top of his pile you place your deck on top of his, which means the king of diamonds is now next to his card.

Finally, when the time comes to announce the cards chosen, the spectator states his and you state yours was (in this example) the king of diamonds. When the spectator looks through the deck he finds that both cards are together as predicted. An easy, but very effective trick you can add to your repertoire.

# THE FAMOUS FOUR ACES TRICK

## Effect

One of the oldest card tricks in the world is the famous Four Aces trick. Every great magician has had his own version of this classic. The following presentation is one that is not dependent on the art of sleight of hand.

Remove the four aces from the deck and shows them to your audience. Turn them face-down and place them on top of the deck. Then deal the aces down onto the table in four different spots. Next, deal three face-down cards on top of each ace. One of the spectators is then requested to pick a pile. You then rap the pile three times with your fist, saying, "Aces, come over!" Then turn the other piles face-up one card at time, saying, "This ace went over! And this ace went over! And finally, this ace went over!"

When you turn over the fourth pile, the chosen one, it's found to contain all four aces. Now let's see how you are going to accomplish this feat.

## Materials needed

One deck of cards.

## Preparation

Prior to presenting the trick remove the four aces, along with any three other cards, and make a pack of them. On the bottom of the pack are the three other cards face-down. On top of these cards are the four aces face-up (Fig. 1). Square

*Fig. 1*

up this packet of seven cards, turn it over, and place it down on the table. The face of one of the other cards is now facing up. Take the rest of the deck, and turning it face-down, bend it inward at the ends. The deck should now have a slight bow in it. Place this deck on top of the small packet on the table. The complete deck should look like Figure 2. In our picture the bow in the deck is exaggerated. Place this deck in a card case and close the flap.

**Fig. 2**

## Presentation

Remove the card case from your pocket, open the flap, and remove the cards face-down. Square the deck and turn it face-up. One of the aces will be showing. Lift off the top seven cards as a single packet. The bow in the rest of the deck, while not being apparent to the audience, will make this move easy. (While holding the deck in your right hand, your left thumb and second and third fingers will feel the edges of the small packet. See Figure 3.) To the audience it

**Fig. 3**

appears that you merely removed a few cards from the bottom of the deck. You then turn over the remainder of the deck and place it on the table.

Square up the cards in your left hand. The top four cards are the aces, face-up. The bottom three cards are the indifferent ones and they are face-down. Tilt the edge of the packet, facing the audience, slightly downwards, so that they can't get an idea of just how many cards are actually in the packet. The right hand now slides the top ace forward while commenting, "I have four aces here. I'm going to turn this ace face-down and place it on the bottom of the packet."

After doing this you slide the next ace off of the packet, saying, "Here's the second ace." You then turn this one over and place it on the bottom of the packet (Fig. 4). You do this

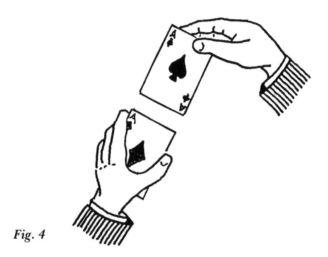

*Fig. 4*

twice more. The top card of the packet is now one of the other face-down cards. However, since you told the audience you had four cards in your hand to start with, they will think that this face-down card is the first ace you turned over.

You now drop the small packet on top of the rest of the deck and you're ready to perform the trick. Deal the top four cards out on the table so that they form a square. The fourth card you put down is the first ace. You now add the next three cards from the top of the deck to it. The four aces are now in this pile. Add three cards to each of the other cards on the table. Put the deck aside and request that one of the spectators give you a number from 1 to 4. No matter what number the spectator selects, you start counting from a pile that will allow you to finish on the pile with the four aces in it. As an example, let's say that the piles are numbered one through four and that the aces are in pile four. If the spectator chooses the number two, then you start counting with pile three. Tap three and say: "One." Then tap pile four and say: "Two." Rap this pile three times, saying, "Aces, come over!" Finally, turn the other three piles face-up to show that the aces have flown, and then turn up the fourth pile and show that the four aces have all come together.

The part of the trick that will need a lot of practice is when you remove the cards from the case and separate the small packet from the rest of the deck. The slight bow in the deck should really make this quite easy. With enough practice this four-ace trick will become one of your favorite card effects.

# A NEW AGE MIND-READING MYSTERY

## Effect

Announce that you have recently discovered the powers of crystals to aid in the transfer of thoughts between individuals. By way of illustration, request that someone from the audience step forward to help in a little experiment. Hand the spectator a deck of cards and ask him to look through it and choose any card and remember it. Then put your hands behind your back and instruct the spectator to place the selected card face-down into your hands. While holding the card behind your back with your left hand, reach into your right pocket with the other hand and bring forth a crystal. Tell the spectator to concentrate on the card that he selected. Call for quiet and gaze intently into the crystal. Eventually, state that the face of the card is materializing in the center of the crystal. First name the color of the card, then the suit, and finally, with great effort, the correct value.

Then bring your left hand from behind your back and show the face of the card to the audience.

Is this another successful experiment in the art of thought transference? Let's find out.

## Materials needed

One deck of cards • one crystal or crystal ball from your local New Age shop.

## Preparation

Either place the crystal in your right jacket pocket or lay it on the table.

## Presentation

There is no forcing of a card in this one. The spectator has a free choice of any card that he wants. When he hands you the card behind your back, insist that the card be face-down. After receiving the card from the spectator have him move forward in front of you so that he can't see your hands behind your back. Tell him to step forward and place the remainder of the deck on the table.

While he is doing this, you quietly tear off one of the two opposite corners of the card that contain the value and suit of the card. Having the card given to you face-down makes it easy to identify which corner to tear off. Palm this small piece of the card under your curled third and little fingers and bring your right hand out from behind your back (Fig. 1). Pick up the crystal from the table, or remove it from

*Fig. 1*

your pocket, and hold it up in front of you in such a way that you can see the small piece of card below it in the palm of your hand (Fig. 2).

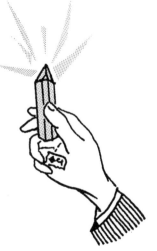

*Fig. 2*

From this point on it's up to you to sell your powers of mind reading to the audience. When the card is revealed, bring your left hand out from behind your back and show the face of the card to the audience. When doing this make sure your thumb and forefingers cover the corner where the piece of card is torn off. In concluding the trick place the card into your left-hand pocket and the crystal, along with the torn piece of card, into your right-hand pocket. Thank the spectator for having such a strong mind and go on to your next miracle.

# FINDING THE REVERSED CARD

## Effect

Remove four court cards from the deck and place them in a row on the table. Then turn around and bid anyone to turn one of the cards 180°. Turn back to the table and pass your hand back and forth over the cards claiming that you can detect the card that was turned around because it will be slightly warmer than the other three cards because it had recently been touched. After a moment or two, stop and pick up one of the cards. It is, of course, the card that had been turned around. Replace the card and proceed to repeat the trick successfully several more times.

## Materials needed

A deck of cards.

## Preparation

Carefully examine the faces of the court cards (the jacks, queens, and kings). What you are looking for are subtle differences in the markings of the figures. Normally the top half of the card is a perfect copy of the bottom half when turned around. However, if you look hard enough you will find small imperfections, or mistakes, which cause these cards to be considered "one way." The more intricate the patterns are, the more possibilities for error.

As an example, the jack of spades in one deck that I checked had in the center of his robes a picture of a spade. If you laid this card down with the point of the spade facing up, it would be easy to detect if it was the card that was turned 180°. The point would then be pointing down.

The jack of diamonds from the same deck had a similar flaw. At the top of the drawing, next to the hand that held a sword, was a row of white diamonds. The points of the diamonds were all visible. However, in the same drawing at the bottom half of the card, the tips of the white diamonds had been cut off. Once again this small difference makes it easy to detect whether the card had been turned or not.

I found similar flaws in three other court cards in the same deck. Once these flaws are known it's easy to spot them. The audience, not being aware that they exist, will wrack their brains trying to determine how you unerringly pick out the card every time.

One thing to note: When you find the card that was turned around, do not just point to it. Pick the card up and turn it so that its face is to the audience. This will enable you to turn the card around so that when you replace it on the table it will once again be aligned the way it was before the spectator turned it. This way the markings on all of the cards will always be in the same positions every time you repeat the trick.

# AN OLD-TIME CARD TRICK

## Effect

The following card trick is really old, and yet it still holds up. It appeared over a hundred years ago in Professor Hoffmann's groundbreaking book *Modern Magic*. Who knows, the good professor may have shown it to the audience that attended his magical soirée back in December 1883, at Tolmers Square Institute in London (Fig. 1). I'll let the professor describe the workings of this card classic to you.

"The problem is to place four kings in different parts of a deck of cards and to bring them back together again by means of a simple cut of the cards. Take the four kings (or any other four cards at pleasure), and exhibit them fanwise (Fig. 2), but secretly place behind the second one (the king of

**Fig. 1**

diamonds in the figure) two other court cards of any description, which, being thus hidden behind the king, will not be visible. The audience being satisfied that the four cards are really the four kings and none other, fold them together and place them at the top of the pack. Draw attention to the

# TOLMERS SQUARE INSTITUTE,

### DRUMMOND STREET, HAMPSTEAD ROAD.

# MAGIC AND MYSTERY

## MONDAY, DECEMBER 24th, 1883,

# By Prof. HOFFMANN,

*(Author of " Modern Magic," &c.)*

Introducing several Original Illusions, never before exhibited in public.

## PROGRAMME.

### +∞ PART I. ∞+

**A CHEMICAL PARADOX.**

" Melted into air--into thin air."—
*The Tempest.*

**AN EXPERIMENT IN THOUGHT-READING.**

" And thought leapt out to wed with thought,
Ere thought could wed itself with speech."—*In Memoriam.*

**THE CHARMED BULLET.**

" A hit—a very palpable hit."—*Hamlet·*

**A HOROLOGICAL EXTRAVAGANZA**

" Call the rest of the watch together."—
*Much Ado about Nothing.*

**A LESSON IN COOKERY.**

" Solid pudding against empty praise."
—*The Dunciad.*

**AN INTERVAL OF TEN MINUTES.**

*(During which Mr. ELEY will deliver a Recitation).*

### +∞ PART II. ∞+

Will consist of a short series of Spiritualistic Illusions (in a new form), in which the Professor's great great grandmother *(Obiit 1763)* is expected to assist. As it will be the old lady's first appearance in Public, and she is rather nervous, it is hoped that she will be treated with proper respect.

*N.B.—No expense has been spared to render this a really attractive Entertainment. The Hall has been swept out for this occasion, and the Hall-keeper has had his hair cut. Notwithstanding these special attractions, the prices of admission will NOT BE RAISED.*

### Further Opinions of the Press and Public as to Prof. Hoffmann's Performances.

" Visitors to the Cattle Show should not fail to see Professor Hoffmann. He is, unquestionably, the fattest conjuror at present before the public."—*Live Stock Gazette.*

" We lent Professor Hoffmann half-a-crown, and he returned it the very same evening. A man like that deserves to be encouraged."—*Financial News.*

" When you ask for Professor Hoffman's entertainment, see that you get it. One trial will suffice. It is the most effectual Kid Reviver ever yet discovered."—*Court Semi-Circular.*

" Professor Hoffmann's entertainment before the Queen of the Andawoman Islands was a tremendous success. There was a little difficulty as to borrowing a pocket-handkerchief, but one of the Court ladies handed up her only garment, which the Professor immediately passed into the Lord Chamberlain's left boot."—*South Sea Islands Advertiser.*

" *To* PROFESSOR HOFFMANN. Sir,—I really do not think you ought to put your great powers to such unwarrantable uses. When I came to your entertainment, I had in my right trousers pocket seven shillings and ninepence-halfpenny ; also a tram ticket, nearly new. When I reached home my pocket was empty. I have instructed my solicitor to issue a county court summons.—Your obedient servant, JONATHAN SLOWCOACH.

" P.S.—I re-open my letter to say it is all right. I have just found the things in my other trousers pocket ;—but please don't do it again."

fact that you are about to distribute these four kings in different parts of the pack. Take the top card, which, being really a king, may be exhibited without apparent intention, and place it at the bottom. Take the next card, which the spectators suppose to be also a king, and place it about halfway down the pack, and the next, in like manner, a little higher. Take the fourth card, which, being actually a king, you may show carelessly, and replace it on the top of the pack. You have now really three kings at the top and one at the bottom, though the audience imagine that they have seen them distributed in different parts of the pack, and are proportionately surprised, when the cards are cut, to find that all the kings are again together.

"It is best to use knaves or queens for the two extra cards, these being less distinguishable from the kings, should a spectator catch a glimpse of their faces."

Thank you, Professor Hoffmann, for sharing that little gem with us. It's always a pleasure to hear from you.

# THE TWENTY-CARD TRICK

## Effect

This is an old but very mystifying card trick. After having a deck of cards shuffled by a member of the audience, deal out ten pairs of cards face-up onto the table. Then request four or five of the spectators to choose mentally any one of the pairs and to memorize the two cards. They do this while your back is turned so you can have no clue as to what pairs have been selected and by whom. Turn around and gather up the cards into a stack. Deal them back onto the table in a very haphazard fashion, making four rows of five cards each. Now proceed to tell the spectators the values of the cards that they mentally selected.

## Materials needed

One deck of playing cards.

## Preparation

You must memorize four simple words and be able to visualize them mentally on the table.

## Presentation

Everything in the above description is true and aboveboard. The only thing you have to do, to accomplish this feat, is to make sure that when you gather up the pairs of cards, after the spectators have made their selections, the cards in the pairs do not become separated. The second thing you have to do, when redealing them to the board, is to place each card of a pair on the same two letters of the following four words:

|   |   |   |   |   |
|---|---|---|---|---|
| G | O | O | S | E |
| A | T | L | A | S |
| R | I | L | E | R |
| T | H | I | G | H |

You must memorize these four words and be able to mentally visualize them printed on the tabletop when you place the twenty cards down. Let's say that you have gathered up the ten pairs of cards and are about to redeal them to the table. The first card, of the first pair, would go on the "G" of *GOOSE*. The second card would go on the "G" of *THIGH*. The first card of the second pair would go on the "A" of *ATLAS* and the second card on the other "A," of *ATLAS*. The first card of the third pair would go on the "S" of *GOOSE* and the second card on the "S" of *ATLAS*. Continue in this manner until all of the cards are down and the audience is presented with four rows of five cards each, all dealt out in an apparent haphazard manner.

To divine the values of any pair chosen, all you have to do is ask the spectator what row or rows the two cards of his pair are in. You then visualize the word, or words, associated with these row(s) and notes which two letters appear in them. (Remember, the four words are made up of ten pairs of letters, and each pair of cards will be found on an individual pair of letters.) The two cards on these letters will be the cards in the pair chosen by the spectator.

In our example the first spectator would say that his cards appear in rows one and four. The only common letters in these two rows are "G." The second would say that his cards appear in row two. Here the only two common letters are "A." In the third example the rows would be one and two. The two common letters here are "S." The cards on these letters correspond to the pairs in question.

Since no one but the members of the audience, who mentally select the pairs, know what cards are involved, the divination of the chosen pairs becomes quite mysterious. They may guess that there is some underlying scheme involved but it is virtually impossible to fathom what it is when you are not in the know. When practising this feat, it is advisable to write out the words on a large sheet of paper and place it on the table. Practice dealing out the cards onto it until their placement becomes second nature.

# THE SPECTATOR FINDS HIS CARD

## Effect

Here's a clever trick where the spectator does all of the work and finds his own chosen card. Hand a deck of cards to a volunteer from the audience and instruct him to remove any ten cards. Next, tell him to mix the cards thoroughly and then to fan them so that only he can see their faces. Have the spectator then mentally select any card in the fan and note its position from the top of the fan. In other words, if he chose the third card from the left, then its position would be three down from the top of the stack when the fan of cards is squared up.

When the selection has been made, have the spectator close the pack and hand it to you. Fan the cards and study their faces. Say, "I know the card you selected mentally, and to prove it I'm going to reveal its identity in an unusual way. I'm going to let you find it for me. Here's the deck. When I turn my back I want you to transfer one card from the top of the stack to the bottom for every position your card is from the top. If your card happens to be fifth from the top, then transfer five cards, one at a time, to the bottom of the pack. Do that now, please!"

After the spectator has complied with these instructions, turn around and say, "Now you're going to find your card. Transfer the top card of the stack to the bottom and place the next card, from the top, onto the table. Continue doing this until you only have one card left in your hand. Do that now, please!"

When the spectator has finished, ask him the value of the card that he mentally selected. After he tells you, say to him, "If you turn over the card in your hand, you will find that you have been left with that very card. How did you do that, anyway?" The spectator turns over the card and shows it to the audience, and then you thank him for his assistance.

## Materials needed

One deck of cards.

## Preparation

None.

## Presentation

The secret to this trick lies in a secret move made after the spectator has mentally selected a card and has returned the stack of ten cards to you. Fan the cards and pretend to divine the chosen card. In so doing, split the fan in two, retaining five cards in each hand. Look first at one set of cards and then at the other. Finally, nod as if to say you now know all, and place the cards back together in one stack. However, in doing this, place the five cards in your left hand under the five cards in your right hand. You do this without changing the original order of any of the cards in either hand. In other words, what you have effectively done is to shift the top five cards of the stack to the bottom. That's all that needs to be done to make this trick work. The rest of the presentation follows the description given above. You can emphasize that it is the spectator who is doing all of the work, and if anyone wishes to know how the trick was done they will jolly well have to ask *him* about it. This is another one of those neat little tricks where the magician can concentrate on the presentation and not worry about finger-flinging.

# A SURPRISING REVELATION

## Effect

Here's a quick trick that's off the beaten path. Remove a deck of cards from its case and shuffle it several times. Then deal out the top eight cards onto the table in a row. Deal all the cards face-down. Ask one of the spectators to point to one of the cards. Move this card to one side and leave it there without turning it face-up. Gather up the remaining cards and place them back on top of the deck.

Then start to deal the cards, one at a time, into a pile on the table. Request the spectator to tell you at any time to stop dealing the cards onto the table. When the spectator does so, put aside the remainder of the deck and pick up the pile you have just made.

"I am now going to deal these cards into a number of piles on the table according to the value of the card you chose when I started this trick." Turn over the face-down card. "The card is the three of clubs, so I'll deal three piles onto the table."

After doing this, comment: "Now let us see what the top card of each of these piles is!" Turn up the top card on each pile. Each one is a three. "Now isn't that a strange thing? After all that shuffling and dealing who would have thought that all four threes would make such an unsuspected appearance? I wonder what the odds are on that ever happening again?"

## Materials needed

One deck of cards.

## Preparation

Before presenting this trick, you need to set up the deck. Remove the four threes and the four fours. Place the four fours on top of the pack and then place the four threes on top of them. Place the cards in the case and you're ready to go.

# Presentation

Remove the cards from the case and shuffle them several times, making sure that the top eight cards remain undisturbed on the top of the deck. Then deal out the top eight cards in a row on the table. Push whichever card is selected to one side. Then pick up the remaining seven cards, going left to right (your left to right). Each card that is picked up goes under the previous cards that have been picked up. When all are off the table, place them back on top of the deck. From the top down, there now are three or four threes and under them three or four fours.

Now start to deal the cards from your pack onto the table into a pile. After you have dealt seven or eight cards, turn to the spectator and say, "I'm making another pile of cards on the table. Please stop me at any time." When the spectator tells you to stop, put aside the remainder of the deck and refer to the face down-card on the table, mentioning that you will redeal the cards into a number of piles according to the value of the chosen card. As the value of the card can only be a three or a four, you will deal them into three or four piles.

We have seen in our above description what happens when the value of the turned-up card is a three. If the value had been a four, then the top card of each of the four piles would have been a three. Either way, the appearance of the four threes is unexpected and unexplainable given all of the shuffling and dealing that the deck has been subject to. This is a nice, quick effect to use at the beginning of your card routine.

# Miscellaneous Items

## A FOLDING MAGIC TABLE

When performing in a parlor or on the stage, you will invariably need one or more tables to hold your apparatus. Any number of professional-type tables can be purchased from the leading magic dealers throughout the country. However, it's always nice to be able to build tables that will accommodate the specific needs of your act. The design we give here is both functional and easy to build. The dimensions will provide you with a large, sturdy table that can be set up or knocked down in seconds. You can, of course, make this table larger or smaller to suit your needs.

The wooden legs are made of 1 × 2-inch stock. The front and side panels are of ⅜-inch cabinet-grade plywood. Fasten the panels to the legs with countersunk screws. Cover the screws with plastic wood and smooth them with sandpaper. Apply glue to all joining surfaces. The sides of the table are fastened to the front of the table with four brass hinges. When completed, paint and decorate to suit your act. Use a white priming undercoat followed by two coats of colored enamel oil paint to give a hard, lasting finish.

The top of the table is half-inch cabinet-grade plywood with four cleats screwed into the bottom. These cleats should be spaced so they engage the top panels of the table sides when they are folded out (Fig. 1). The cleats should be short enough so they fit between the two legs of each side panel. The tabletop effectively locks the table together. The tabletop is painted like the rest of the table, using an undercoat followed by two coats of enamel paint. An alternative finish on the top side of the tabletop is a piece of black velvet. Tack it along the edges of the table and then cover the edges with strips of gold cloth tape.

To get a better idea of colors and designs check out the tables on sale at your local magic shop. Also, take note the

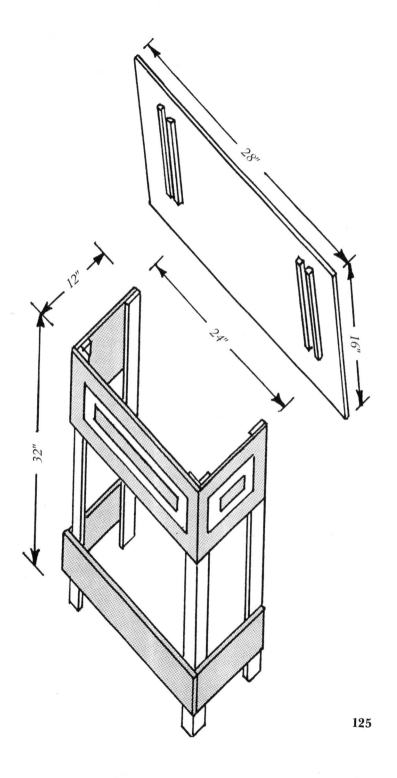

next time you see a magic show on television. The table pictured here is light in weight and easily knocks down for carrying. The two side panels fold in against the front of the table (Fig. 2). This also makes for easy storage.

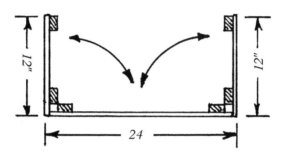

**Fig. 2**

# ABOUT THE AUTHOR

Charles Barry Townsend has been writing books dealing with puzzles, games and magic for 25 years. He is the author of 20 books, including *The World's Best Magic Tricks, The World's Most Incredible Puzzles, The World's Hardest Puzzles, The World's Most Amazing Puzzles, The World's Greatest Puzzles,* and *Great Victorian Puzzle Book,* all published by Sterling Publishing Company. Mr. Townsend lives in Mill Creek, Washington, where he spends a good deal of his time thinking up ways to confound and entertain readers like you.

Pictured below are the author and his dog, Jackie, studying a poster used by the greatest magician of all time, Mr. Harry Houdini. If you check the Paper Magic section of this book you will find an explanation by Mr. Houdini of the famous "Paper Bird of Japan" trick.

# INDEX